The Business of
HR in Business Schools

The Business of HR in Business Schools

V R K Prasad

Viva Books

New Delhi | Mumbai | Chennai | Kolkata | Bengaluru | Hyderabad | Kochi | Guwahati

Publisher's note

Every possible effort has been made to ensure that the information contained in this book is accurate at the time of going to press, and the publisher and author cannot accept responsibility for any errors or omissions, however caused. No responsibility for loss or damage occasioned to any person acting, or refraining from action, as a result of the material in this publication can be accepted by the editor, the publisher or the author.

Every effort has been made to trace the owners of copyright material used in this book. The author and the publisher will be grateful for any omission brought to their notice for acknowledgement in the future editions of the book.

First Published 2011

Viva Books Private Limited

- 4737/23, Ansari Road, Daryaganj, New Delhi 110 002
  Tel. 42242200, 23258325, 23283121, Email: vivadelhi@vivagroupindia.net
- 76, Service Industries, Shirvane, Sector 1, Nerul, Navi Mumbai 400 706
  Tel. 27721273, 27721274, Email: vivamumbai@vivagroupindia.net
- Jamals Fazal Chambers, 26 Greams Road, Chennai 600 006
  Tel. 28294241, 28290304, Email: vivachennai@vivagroupindia.net
- B-103, Jindal Towers, 21/1A/3 Darga Road, Kolkata 700 017
  Tel. 22816713, Email: vivakolkata@vivagroupindia.net
- 7, GF, Sovereign Park Aptts., 56-58, K. R. Road, Basavanagudi, Bengaluru 560 004
  Tel. 26607409, Email: vivabangalore@vivagroupindia.net
- 101-102, Moghal Marc Apartments, 3-4-637 to 641, Narayanguda, Hyderabad 500 029
  Tel. 27564481, Email: vivahyderabad@vivagroupindia.net
- First Floor, Beevi Towers, SRM Road, Kaloor, Kochi 682 018
  Tel. 0484-2403055, 2403056, Email: vivakochi@vivagroupindia.net
- 232, GNB Road, Beside UCO Bank, Silpukhuri, Guwahati 781 003
  Tel. 0361-2666386, Email: vivaguwahati@vivagroupindia.net

www.vivagroupindia.com

ISBN: 978-81-309-1734-4

Published by Vinod Vasishtha for Viva Books Private Limited, 4737/23 Ansari Road, Daryaganj, New Delhi 110 002.

Printed & bound by Sanat Printers, Kundli 131 028.

M0200/M0450

Dedicated to
my mother, Smt Vemuri Jayalakshmi,
an embodiment of
love and affection

A University stands for humanism, for tolerance, for reason, for the adventure of ideas and for the search for truth. It stands for the onward march of the human race towards even higher objectives. If the universities discharge their duties adequately then it is well with the nation and the people.

– Pandit Jawaharlal Nehru

The future of the HRD movement is in realizing that we have not even touched the most important sectors like education, health, infrastructure, government etc. where HR interventions are most needed. We need to pay attention to these strategic sectors. The spirit of HRD lies in learning from each other: teachers, managers, doctors, nurses, in fact all citizens 'involved' in the pursuit of change and development.

– Udai Pareek and TV Rao

Contents

Foreword

Recognizing the importance of Human Resources Development at all levels, the United Nations Development Program (UNDP) has been publishing Human Development Reports since the last two decades. The HDR gives details of the extent to which the people in each country can be considered as developed. Put in a simple way, those countries that have people who manage to live longer are considered as well-developed countries in terms of the human resources. To live longer you should have a quality of life and purchasing power. To have purchasing power you should have knowledge and skill base. All the three indices are taken to form a Human Development Index (HDI). These are computed by putting together indices of life expectancy at birth, mean years of schooling and other indices of skill development and per capita income equated for parity in purchasing power. In all this, education is a critical component. Schools, Colleges, Universities and other institutions of education constitute a significant source that influences all the three components of human development.

Recent experiences have shown that business schools have a special role to play in this. In certain ways the business school produced people are responsible for economic upliftment of the nations or downturn of the economies as shown by the recession a couple of years ago. Whether these are business schools or not, it is the education systems and the way they are managed that determine the efficiency and effectiveness of the human resources in a country.

Without human development there is no economic development in a sustainable way. Thus management education occupies an important role in the nation's development. With this increasing relevance of management education, visionary leaders like Pandit Nehru as Prime Minister of India and a scientist and institution builder Dr. Vikram Sarabhai laid the foundation for starting institutions like the IIMA and IIMC. In the private sector, visionary Jesuits devoted to education started institutions like the XLRI.

HRM is taught in these institutions as a part of the MBA curriculum or as separate stream of specialization. When it is offered as a stream of specialization these institutions produce HR managers who are supposed to influence and impact the lives of numerous employees that serve different organizations in various forms.

The credibility of management schools is often determined by the extent to which they practice what they preach. Hence in a subject like HRM or HRD, the students and participants become extremely sensitive if the institution where they study does not have right practices and does not attempt to practice what they preach.

Management schools are under close scrutiny by its participants for their credibility. Hence it is important that these schools pay adequate attention to the way they manage themselves.

Institution builders like Ravi Matthai, Udai Pareek, Dharni Sinha, Nitish De, KRS Murthy devoted a lot of time designing the processes and systems to manage business school effectively. Key among the Institutional processes is HR practices followed.

Such HR practices cover the way the faculty are recruited, socialized, evaluated, developed, motivated and encouraged to influence the students and others who go through the systems and build them as leaders and change agents. Faculty recruitment, evaluation and development are key issues in the HRM of Educational Institutions. Institutional culture occupies even better and more important role in motivating, inspiring and developing the faculty and through them the students.

Prior to my joining IIMA in 1973, I had the opportunity to work at two Universities and one Central Government Institution. These three Institutions offered three different cultures and contexts. In the Universities we worked, we were the first to start the department of Psychology. We had all the freedom to set values and culture within the University system but no budgets. We created values and systems where learning was always the focus. The first example was set by the faculty who used to work much more than what they expected their students to work. But they were all hierarchy driven systems.

It was for the first time at IIMA, I found that when I joined in 1973 there was a culture where even a fresh recruit or a junior faculty was trusted and given high importance. Whether you were an Assistant Professor or Professor or Chair Professor, you were called a "professor" and had the same privileges like the office room, shared secretarial services and residential accommodations comparable to the senior faculty. So the faculty energies were focused on making an impact and getting good feedback from students, doing quality research and be considered as an outstanding teacher. So the HR practices in terms of developing a HRD culture were set by the head of the Institution. There was great planning a few months in advance for the coming year. Commitments had to be honored. Faculty were encouraged to do consultancy but recognized not for how much consultancy they had done but for the kind of knowledge they brought into the classroom through their publications and case studies.

There are many institutions like the IIMs that have great HRM practices. As there are over a thousand Management schools and several colleges and universities it is necessary to study and document the same. Unfortunately no such attempt seems to have been made in the past. Dr. (Col) Prasad has done a great service to the education field in bringing out this book covering various aspects of HRM in management schools. The book covers recruitment, selection, performance appraisal, development and culture building aspects.

I am sure this book will be well appreciated and found very useful by all Heads of Institutions and Universities.

I wish a pleasant reading and a great practice for all those who manage institutions of higher education.

TV Rao
Chairman, TVRLS;
Founder President,
National HRD Network
Adjunct Professor, IIMA

Ahmedabad
January 2011

Preface

Close to three decades in the army followed by yet another one in academics developed a keen interest in me for the people dimension of organizations. Every manager irrespective of the discipline he pursues basically needs to be a people manager first. With liberalization of the economy, the Indian industry is poised for a major growth despite the recession all over. Thus there is a dire need to upgrade ourselves to global standards as we move from industrial economy to knowledge economy. Organizations can achieve competitive edge only when they further move to innovation economy where effective use of the skills of its people is made. Creating, disseminating, acquiring and using knowledge as a process is going to assume significance hitherto unknown to mankind. We are living in a knowledge driven era.

Human resources in India have catapulted suddenly to attract the attention of the entire world as the key to further development. HR is a value adder, performance enhancer and finally it delivers results—a proposition which needs no further debate. It has come a long way from its 'compliance' days to 'commitment', which is a force that binds an individual to a course of action relevant to the objective. The existing literature on sector specific HRM is vague and a little fragmented too, to say the least. Though fundamental issues may remain the same generally, yet they would vary significantly, say in a 'service industry' as against an R&D outfit. Effective HRM practices are especially important for service organizations where the satisfaction of the employee can influence the quality of service provided and the organization's ability to retain employees (Murphy 2003; Ulrich 1997; Voss, Tsikriktsis, Funk, Yarrow and Owen 2005). Education accounts for more than $ 3 billion of the world's economy. The General Agreement on Trade in Services (GATS) included 'education' as a service.

Early months of the year 2000 saw me making an entry as faculty in a well known business school of the country where I started delving deeply into the theoretical aspects of HRM having seen the practical side of it in the army. I have seen this school, over the last decade, growing from strength to strength to become one of the largest business schools in the world including attaining the status of a 'deemed to be university'. Over the years, while teaching HRM and OB to postgraduate and doctoral level students, including raising an exclusive HR school, there was always a lack of conviction in me as I noticed wide gaps between preaching and practice. HRM practices in use were more by default than by design. A casual survey revealed that situation is no different in other famous business schools of the country. This led me to adopt a more focused approach towards the issue by undertaking a study of HRM practices in business schools, which culminated in receiving the award of a doctoral degree from a well known university of the country. My observation got further cemented by Taylor's (1994) findings that senior managers in industry believe that business schools do not practice what they preach in terms of utilizing best practices and that they need to be more proactive in becoming transformational organizations. Given the 'service' nature of business schools as educational institutions, their effectiveness depends upon how they address the needs of multiple constituencies both internal and external to their organizations such as faculty, staff, students and the business community. Faculty and staff in particular play a critical role as the major service providers, representing the face of the business school in their interactions with students and the business community (Nancy Day and Joy Peluchette 2006).

India is reported to be the largest producer of management graduates in the world next only to US that too at a cost which is a fraction of what it is elsewhere in the world. That the management education is vital for the growth of any country is an irrefutable fact, but the issue is delivery of a 'quality' management education. This quality will come only through quality faculty, their development and good governance of business schools. Business Schools in India have the sacred responsibility of turning out not only competent and socially conscious managers but those who could give Indian business a global boost by meeting any challenge and by coping up with the changing demands.

Given the above situation, it was prudent to examine the way the stakeholder groups are managed, particularly the faculty. A lot of emphasis was laid on rankings or accreditation whose focus was on curricula, infrastructure and placement, etc. While faculty's qualifications, research and publications were considered as parameters but sadly none took into account any other HR issues like their compensation, PMS, training or motivation, etc.

Unfortunately this led to a state where the administrators of business schools neither paid any explicit attention to HR practices themselves, nor employed any exclusive HR functionary to address the issues. Frustration among faculty was only a natural manifestation when they teach something which they cannot practice themselves or when their students get impressive salary packages after graduation as compared to what they get. This glaring disconnection made me think and undertake the onerous task of writing this book based on my research work and having glanced over the extent to which HRM practices are being put to use in a cross section of business schools across the country, specially the ones in the private sector that we have large numbers. The aim is to provide a 'one point reference guide' to all the heads of such business schools who value use of effective HRM practices and consider faculty as a vibrant and vital part of the organization always committed to its success and growth, more so because they enjoy more functional freedom in implementing the practices discussed and suggested, in comparison to those heading the state run institutions.

Dr V R K Prasad

Acknowledgements

This book is a culmination of all ideas and thoughts collected through my intellectual journey over a decade with the Institute of Chartered Financial Analysts of India spearheaded by Mr. NJ Yasaswy, to whom I wish to express a deep sense of gratitude for igniting the academic spark and for reposing tremendous faith and trust, in me.

I am deeply indebted to Dr. Gopu Venkatswamy, my guide during research with Osmania University, Hyderabad, which formed the basis for this book. I am thankful to my colleagues in ISHRD, Professors Varaprasad, Showry and Narendar for their help in the compilation, and my special thanks to Brig Deshpande, Former Director, XVJIM, Hyderabad for his valuable suggestions on my manuscript, and I did address them.

I owe appreciation thanks to the revered gurus of HR, Professors Udai Pareek and TV Rao, the former for guiding and encouraging me to undertake this onerous task, and the latter for going through the manuscript and contributing the 'Foreword'. Thanks also for the very valuable suggestions that got implemented.

To my colleagues Ankur and more to Arnavaz, who painstakingly converted my difficult manuscripts into readable fonts. Thanks for giving the book its present shape.

Special thanks to the various authors of books, article writers and others from the academic fraternity from whose works I borrowed a lot who were cited formally to the extent possible and my apologies to those left out inadvertently. Nevertheless I appreciate and value their work.

I would like to make a special mention of my wife Durga who has been a constant source of inspiration for me. I thank her for putting up with my long hours on the computer.

Lastly, I am grateful to my parents and the great God Almighty as I owe everything in me to them and also for giving me the strength to undertake and complete this book.

Dr V R K Prasad

Introduction

Human Resource is one of the most valuable assets of an organization. Megginson terms human resources as 'the total knowledge, skills, creative abilities, talents and aptitudes of an organization's workforce as well as the values, attitudes and beliefs of the individuals involved'. Human Resource Management (HRM) is one of the most complex and challenging fields of management. Management as a process involves, planning, organizing, staffing, leading and controlling activities that facilitate the achievement of an organization's objectives. Human Resource Management deals with the people dimension in management. Byars and Rue say that 'Human Resources Management encompasses those activities designed to provide for and co-ordinate the human resources of an organization'. According to Ivancevich and Glueck, 'Personnel/ Human Resource Management is the function performed in organizations that facilitate the most effective use of people (employees) to achieve organizational and individual goals.'

Every organization is composed of people and utilizing their services, developing their skills, motivating them to enhance their levels of performance and ensuring that they remain committed to the organization are essential for the accomplishment of organizational objectives. This is true for all types of organizations—government, business, education, health, recreation or social action. Acquiring and retaining good human resources is an essential precondition for the success of every organization.

HRM is a process that consists of four main functions—acquiring, developing, motivating and retaining human resources. The acquisition function starts with planning (for the categories and number of employees required) and ends with staffing. The development function has three dimensions, employee training, skill enhancement and career development. The motivation function includes identifying individual motivational needs of employees and finding ways to meet them. The retention function is concerned with providing a conducive work environment to the employees and nurturing them to make them feel committed and attached to the organization. These functions and their constituent sub-functions have changed over the years in response to changes in the social and political environment of business and also as a result of fresh developments in management thought.

Now the question arises 'are the management education institutions or for that matter any educational institutions different from any business enterprise, in expecting effective performance from its employees'? The answer is a simple 'no'. The difference is rather minute, to the extent that the objective is commercial in case of a business enterprise while it is the quality of student output that is of concern in an educational institution. If this is the case then human resource management in an educational institution is as important as it is in any business enterprise. This aspect assumes all the more significance in a management education institute where the subject is taught to the prospective managers and no teaching can be effective unless it is practiced by the teachers themselves. HRM as a functional discipline is generally a taken-for-granted field more so in an educational institution. India has carved a niche for itself in the management education field as one of the largest producers of management graduates in the world. But the large number of institutions have been causing erosion in the quality of faculty and students which could be an offshoot of the poor state of human resource management practices in these institutions. Thus there is an urgent need to take a critical look at this aspect.

Most graduating students find management education as a popular choice for higher education because of its interdisciplinary approach and the rising job opportunities for MBAs. To meet the rising demand there has been a rapid expansion of business schools in India especially in the last decade and a half. The unintended consequence of this sharp increase in MBA schools is the steep erosion in the quality of management education. In spite of model curriculum designed by AICTE there is a wide variation in the quality of business schools, as some are truly world class and richly endowed while others are merely teaching shops. By and large business schools have not been able to bring a world of reality to the classroom. This development while satisfying the market demand for management education has also become debatable among management experts, students, academicians and corporate groups, on the purpose of these institutions and their concern for quality education. The MBA graduates produced by these institutions are also being carefully assessed on their employability by the corporate sector.

In the light of circumstances enumerated above, it is opined that there is an urgent need to take a close look at the very 'makers' of the managers in the first place. HRM as a core discipline forms an essential ingredient of the curriculum with specialization also being available. The question is whether the concepts that are taught being practiced at all? That is at the institutional level itself. Sadly HRM despite its relevance and importance to every organization is yet to find a place for itself in educational institutions. The reason could be social, cultural or even historic. Since teaching as a profession in India is unfortunately rarely considered worthy of pursuit. Except the periodic business school ranking surveys that have been commenting on the general state of HRM particularly about the quality of the faculty, not much specific work has been done to bring home certain vital and more important aspects of HR. Managements of business schools are under constant pressure to find right ways and means to attract, develop, motivate and retain faculty and staff. So far no comprehensive study appears to have been undertaken in this regard and hence this effort of compilation.

The book is divided into two parts. Part I has three chapters. Chapter 1 provides an overview of management education in general with special reference to its present status in India. In Chapter 2, the relevance of HRM practices in business schools is discussed in detail with focus on ideal state of affairs on HRM front. Chapter 3 briefly touches upon the existing literature in the area.

Part II has eight chapters, wherein each chapter deals with a particular HRM function. We start with 'acquisition' function in Chapter 4 where various methods of recruiting and selecting faculty are discussed. Providing adequate skill developmental facilities is yet another important HR activity which is discussed in Chapter 5 suitably titled as Training and Development. Knowledge creation is as important as its dissemination in institutions of higher learning and a full Chapter 6 is devoted to research, publication and consulting by faculty. Performance management was rather a non-priority activity in many schools under our study, and hence a need was felt to discuss this at length in Chapter 7. Though the compensation levels in most of the state-run business schools/university departments have improved with the VI pay commission recommendations under AICTE fold and UGC pay revision committee proposals, but they are still a far cry in most of the privately run business schools of which we have plenty and for whom the book is mainly meant. These issues are addressed in Chapter 8. Organizational climate and culture depend a lot on morale and motivation of the staff and business school faculty is no exception to this rule, and Chapter 9 takes a close look at this vital component of HRM. Little or no purpose would be served if sound HRM practices are put in place without paying adequate attention to faculty retention strategies and their separation process. The penultimate Chapter 10 deals with these issues. Chapter 11 highlights the all important aspects of business school leadership and its governance.

As I understand, the book is a maiden attempt in this vital but otherwise a very sensitive area. The aim is to help the business school fraternity in improving their lot and in the process improve the state and the quality of management education in the country. Errors and omissions if any are unintended and suggestions are always welcome. The book very briefly touches upon the HRM issues of non-teaching staff under the assumption that they would be taken care of by the institutional heads in the same lines as they do for the faculty. Needless to say that the views expressed in the book are purely personal and the methods discussed are suggestive only in nature.

Abbreviations

AACSB	:	Association to Advance Collegiate Schools of Business
AAPBS	:	Association of Asia-Pacific Business Schools
ABID-MS	:	All India Board of Management Studies
AICTE	:	All India Council for Technical Education
AIMA	:	All India Management Association
AIMS	:	Association of Indian Management Schools
AMBA	:	Association of MBAs
AMDISA	:	Association of Management Development Institutions in South Asia
AP	:	Achievement Press
ASCI	:	Administrative Staff College of India
ASTD	:	American Society for Training and Development
CAT	:	Common Admission Test
CEO	:	Chief Executive Officer
CL	:	Collegial Leadership
CPI	:	Consumer Price Index
CI	:	Continuous Improvement
CSR	:	Corporate Social Responsibility
COSMODE	:	Consortium for Strategic Management and Organization Development
ECCH	:	European Case Clearing House
EEP	:	Executive Education Program

EFMD	:	European Foundation for Management Development
EQUIS	:	European Quality Improvement System
FDI	:	Foreign Direct Investment
FDPs	:	Faculty Development Programs
FMS	:	Faculty of Management Studies
FPG	:	Friend, Philosopher and Guide
GDP	:	Gross Domestic Product
HBS	:	Harvard Business School
HOD	:	Head of the Department
HRA	:	House Rent Allowance
HR	:	Human Resources
HRM	:	Human Resource Management
HRP	:	Human Resource Planning
IBS	:	Icfai Business School
ICBM	:	Institute of Computers and Business Management
ICFAI	:	Institute of Chartered Financial Analysts of India
IIM	:	Indian Institute of Management
IIMT	:	Icfai Institute for Management Teachers
IIPM	:	Indian Institute of Planning and Management
IISc	:	Indian Institute of Science
IIT	:	Indian Institute of Technology
IMT	:	Institute of Management Technology
INC	:	Icfai National College
IPE	:	Institute of Public Enterprise
IPR	:	Intellectual Property Rights
ISB	:	Indian School of Business
ISO	:	International Organization for Standardization
IT	:	Information Technology
ITES	:	Information Technology Enabled Services
ITM	:	Institute for Technology and Management

IV	:	Institutional Vulnerability
JNTU	:	Jawaharlal Nehru Technological University
KAP	:	Knowledge, Application and Personality
KPI	:	Key Performance Indicators
LBS	:	London Business School
MAO-C	:	Motivational Analysis of Organizations-Climate
MBA	:	Masters in Business Administration
MDI	:	Management Development Institute
MIT	:	Massachusetts Institute of Technology
MNCs	:	Multi National Corporations
MS	:	Master of Science
NAAC	:	National Assessment and Accreditation Council
NBA	:	National Board of Accreditation
NGOs	:	Non-Governmental Organizations
NICOM	:	Nirma's International Conferences in Management
NIM	:	Nirma Institute of Management
NIT	:	National Institute of Technology
NKC	:	National Knowledge Commission
OCDQ	:	Organizational Climate Description Questionnaire
OCI	:	Organizational Climate Index
PGDM	:	Postgraduate Diploma in Management
PMS	:	Performance Management System
PSE	:	Perceived Self-Efficacy
PTB	:	Professional Teacher Behaviour
QA	:	Quality Assurance
QIP	:	Quality Improvement Program
REC	:	Regional Engineering College
R&D	:	Research and Development
R&S	:	Recruitment and Selection

SAQS	:	South Asian Quality Systems
SFP	:	Self Fulfilling Prophecy
T&D	:	Training and Development
TISCO	:	Tata Iron and Steel Company
TISS	:	Tata Institute of Social Sciences
TQM	:	Total Quality Management
UCLA	:	University of California, Los Angeles
UGC	:	University Grants Commission
UK	:	United Kingdom
USA	:	United States of America
US	:	United States
VFM	:	Value for Money
XLRI	:	Xavier's Labour Relations Institute

PART I

1

An Overview of Management Education in India

Management education is the process of learning values, attitudes, information and skills to achieve desired relations between resources and objectives.

– NR Chaudhury (2001)

BRIEF GLOBAL HISTORY

Management education has never been so much in focus and assumed such critical importance as in these times of global competition and recession. This global scenario is changing the relationship between management education and business. The global management education is estimated to be US $22 billion (Friga, Bettis and Sullivan 2003) and is reported to be growing at about 10 to 12 per cent per annum. USA is leading the pack with about 900 Universities offering masters in management (Pfeffer and Long 2002).

Businessman Joseph Wharton was the pioneer of the first bachelors program in business in 1881 in the University of Pennsylvania (Wharton School of Finance and Commerce). Universities of Chicago and California followed suit in 1898. Dartmouth College was reportedly the first school to offer masters degree in business in 1900. Formal MBA (Master of Business Administration) program made its beginning in Harvard University (HBS) in 1908 closely followed by Stanford in 1925 (Henry Mintzberg). There are other schools of thought which say that the first management education program was started at MIT in 1931 and Harvard followed it in 1943 (SL Rao 2005). University of Pennsylvania published the first review in business education in 1931 (McFarland 1960), and Carnegie Foundation came out with its report on management education in 1959 (Pierson 1959) both highlighting the weaknesses in management education, resulting in the establishment of accreditation bodies like Association to Advance Collegiate Schools of Business (AACSB), European Quality Improvement System (EQUIS), European Foundation for Management Development (EFMD), South Asian Quality Systems (SAQS), Association of Asia-Pacific Business Schools (AAPBS) and Association of MBAs (AMBA) that facilitated management education to improve and grow rapidly thereafter to bring it to what it is today world over.

MANAGEMENT EDUCATION IN INDIA

The end of colonial era and the dawn of independence brought in a new role for the education. The then Prime Minister Pandit Jawaharlal Nehru decided to create centers of academic excellence outside the university system and the efforts bore fruits in the shape of IITs, IIMs and NITs (erstwhile RECs). While the universities numbering in excess of 300 have played a vital role in higher education, the contribution of IITs and IIMs in enlarging the pool of educated manpower is equally praiseworthy. Report of the first education commission envisaged a much greater role for the education in modernization of the country. As rightly expected there has been a phenomenal expansion of higher education in India. With this the developmental concerns in the country have also undergone a paradigm shift focusing more on human resources development than on economic development.

Education and management are inseparable twins. The difference generally lies only in the application of relevant techniques. The 9th plan focused on educational management a concept which got reiterated in the 10th plan. During the last decade or so Indian business moved from regulation to deregulation, from state control to private initiative, from domestic focus to global, all under the pressure of globalization. This change augmented by IT, Internet and recognition of human capital as the vital resource of new economy, has caused a paradigm shift in management education. The challenges of globalization necessitated application of sound management principles in every enterprise. It has caused higher educational institutions, more so the management institutes, to look at international business and focus on producing graduates with global mindsets, rather than just turning out any graduate. The advent of technology and the rising popularity of Internet are altering the traditional models of education delivery promoting interactive communication, etc. The knowledge economy has brought the importance of human capital to the forefront and their skills are becoming vital in management education. The competitive advantage of our nation lies in our human capital. With the vast pool of professional and technical manpower we have, the knowledge economy is likely to generate wealth for the nation. Thus there is a strong need to nurture high quality educational institutions in the country. The hallmark of higher education lies not only in dissemination of knowledge but in its creation too which is going to be a bigger challenge in the coming days. This calls for a conducive climate of scholarship and access to funds (Dharni Sinha 2004).

Management education is comparatively a young academic discipline to arrive in the world of academia, barely a century old. It is in its fifties as far as the Indian sub-continent is concerned making it a post-independence phenomenon. The Indian Institute of Science (IISc) at Bangalore started a program in Industrial Management in 1948. This was followed by a part time PG Diploma program in 1954 by Indian Institute of Social Welfare and Business Management, Kolkata. Administrative Staff College of India (ASCI) introduced executive education in Management in 1956. All India Management Association (AIMA), a professional body for the promotion of management as a discipline in general and of management education in particular, was started in 1957. The Andhra University at Visakhapatnam, Andhra Pradesh was reportedly the first to start a full time postgraduate management program in 1957. Delhi University followed up with their programs in 1958. A number of universities came up with postgraduate programs in management thereafter, mostly offering three year part time courses for working executives. The University of Madras, University of Jodhpur, University of Allahabad, Punjab University and Bombay University set up their Masters in Business Administration (MBA) program in the 1960s. Majority of the universities set up their management programs between 1970 and 1995.

In 1959 George W Robbins, Associate Dean, Graduate School of Business Administration, University of California, Los Angeles, was invited at the instance of the Planning Commission through the good offices of Ford Foundation to recommend an educational program for management. The report of Dean, Robbins recommended the following:

"An Institute of Management should be established on an All-India basis. It must be regarded as a high priority national asset indispensable in the development of the resources of management, i.e. the manpower to translate natural resources, technology and human talent into effective organizations to produce wealth. Accordingly it must receive financial support from industry and government, adequate for its needs in a planned and phased development. Further, that the institute should be a postgraduate center of teaching and research where attention is focused on the most difficult problems of management rather than on the routine of business practices and where education and training include the acquisition of knowledge, attitude and skills of management in business."

The report was accepted by the Government of India and it was decided to set up two institutes, one in Calcutta (now Kolkata) and the other in Ahmedabad. The first ever Indian Institute of Management was set up in Kolkata in November 1961 in collaboration with Alfred P Sloan School of Management of MIT, USA. The Institute at Ahmedabad was established in June 1962 in collaboration with Harvard Business School, USA. Later seven more Institutes of Management were set-up at Bangalore (1972), Lucknow (1984) and at Indore and Kozhikode in 1997 Shillong in 2008, Ranchi in 2009, and Tiruchirapalli in 2010.

These All India Institutes were set up as autonomous societies in the Ministry of Education with funding from the central government. Despite their dependence for funding on the government, IIMs enjoyed functional freedom in terms of faculty recruitment and curriculum design, international collaboration, etc. The entry of private operators began with the setting up of Xavier's Labour Relations Institute (XLRI) in 1966 at Jamshedpur with the active support of Tata Iron and Steel Company (TISCO). Then came up the SP Jain Institute Management & Research at Mumbai and Management Development Institute (MDI) at Gurgaon that now are a part of the elite league alongside IIMs and Faculty of Management Studies (FMS), Delhi University. By the early nineties close to 120 universities in the country had set up their full-fledged departments of business management and started offering management programs. However, the demand for management education far outnumbered the supply and post-1990 era witnessed mushrooming growth of these institutes mostly in the private sector.

GROWTH

Economists believe the growth in management education is a barometer of growth in economy of the country.

– Dharni P Sinha (2004)

Management education is barely 50 years old in India. The Andhra University at Visakhapatnam, Andhra Pradesh, was reportedly the first to start management program in 1957. Subsequently it registered a phenomenal growth spreading its tentacles all over the country. What began as a preserve of the elite, is now available to the students of poor families too. Thanks to the liberalized education loan facilities extended by the government through banks. The Indian Institutes of Management at Kolkata, Ahmedabad, Bangalore, Indore, Kozhikode, Shillong, Ranchi and Tiruchirapalli were subsequently set up by the government between 1961 and 2010. However, following a comprehensive exercise carried out by the Government of India on the national education policy in 1986 an autonomous body to promote develop and supervise technical education (including management education) was created called All India Council for Technical Education (AICTE) under an act of Parliament in 1987. As the IIMs at Kolkata and Ahmedabad began their operations many universities retrofitted their commerce departments and carved out departments of management and started offering MBA programs. However there were a couple of exceptions such as University of Delhi and University of Punjab which established separate faculty of management. By the early nineties, close to 80 university based departments of management were functioning in the country, and this number soon rose to 120. It was at this juncture, the state encouraged establishment of private funded business schools to meet the excess demand for management graduates and strengthened AICTE with the twin responsibilities of maintaining/upgrading the standards of management education and regulating all business schools in the country. AICTE granted permission liberally to establish new business schools. The number of such institutions increased phenomenally by the year 2002. As of now these postgraduate management programs are run by societies, trusts, university departments and affiliated colleges. AICTE in 1998 decided to discontinue PGDM program undertaken by autonomous societies and encouraged them to affiliate with the existing universities.

Recent surveys of business schools, however, have shown that the PGDM offered by autonomous societies including IIMs have done far better than the university programs (Dharni Sinha 2005).

MBA and PGDM education currently are available through residential, full time and distance mode. All of them add up to close to 2000 programs including sectoral ones; while some of them are approved by the AICTE and the rest are on their own stream provided by the acceptance from the industry. In addition, there are a large number of foreign universities which offer management education in the country either independently or as a joint venture with Indian business schools. With the entry of transnational organizations and globalization of economies the demand for management graduates having overseas degrees has been increasing. To attract high salary for their graduates coupled with an opportunity to work in globally oriented corporations, many business schools are joining hands with foreign counterparts by turning out MBAs who supposedly receive overseas management education within India.

Most of the quantitative expansion in the management education in the last decade (2000–2010) has come in the private domain. This has been partly because of the strict entry barriers of the public funded elite business schools like IIMs while university departments could rarely respond to the growing market needs, with their limited resources. Yet another reason is the financial viability and attraction in opening and running a business school. Entry of the private operators in the management education in India is a kind of milestone in its history since some of them have become the best business schools in the country.

The rise of management education in India is meteoric and as of now even sky is not the limit. The market for sectoral management education is slowly but surely emerging and soon India will have exclusive schools offering MBA program in all disciplines viz, finance, marketing, information technology, telecom, human resources, banking, insurance, forestry, tourism, hospitality, entrepreneurship, family business, agriculture, co-operatives, rural plantation, healthcare, retail and education to name a few.

THE NEW EQUATION: RANKING SURVEYS

Undoubtedly India's IIMs have established themselves by finding places in the top 100 best institutes of the world; but this is only one side of the story. The fact is, just about a quarter of one lakh odd management graduates coming out of, close to, 2000 institutes are reportedly employable. Quantity has compromised the quality as mushrooming growth and proliferation of management institutes was noticed in the last 10–15 years. Rightly stepped in Consortium for Strategic Management and Organization Development (COSMODE) which introduced the first ever business school rankings in the country in 1988, and there has been no looking back since then. Business schools stepped up and started responding to the rankings and the issues raised there in. However, university departments lagged behind and took no particular action, due to reasons beyond the control of the faculty or the heads of the departments who themselves were keen to bring about changes.

During the last decade Indian business has witnessed unprecedented change due to liberalization, privatization and globalization. This was further augmented by the technological advancements in Information Technology (IT), Internet and telecom fields and recognition of the human capital as the driver of new economy. This has caused a paradigm shift in management education. MBAs would now have to learn about brand value and Intellectual Property Rights (IPR) and patents apart from just concentrating on profits, costs and competition alone. Internet is altering the very concept of education delivery and IT has now become an integral part of management education. Next is the knowledge economy which has brought the 'human capital' to the forefront which further resulted in inclusion of topics on leadership, teamwork, entrepreneurship, risk taking, conflict management, attitude, motivation, service orientation, change in mindset, flexibility and other related soft skills as the main ingredients of curriculum for imparting effective management education. Finally the changing business scenario has caused a major shift from manufacturing to service economy and hence the reorientation of the management programs to the changing needs. Professional bodies like All India Management Association (AIMA), Association of Indian Management Schools (AIMS) (1988) and Association of Management Development Institutions in South Asia (AMDISA) (1988) have been doing pioneering work to promote the cause of management education in India by associating themselves with the business press in carrying out business school ranking surveys. Business Today, Business India, Business World, Outlook and Economic Times normally undertake ranking surveys on annual basis using generally the same parameters to judge the business schools under survey. Though the top-rung schools like the IIMs, FMS Delhi, SP Jain Institute of Management & Research, Mumbai, Management Development Institute (MDI), Gurgaon, and XLRI at Jamshedpur retain their positions (give and take a couple of notches), it is the second rung business schools that get hyper activated by these rankings. Rightly so, because Indian industry get maximum of its managerial talent requirements met by these institutions, as Multi National Corporations (MNCs) generally go in for students from the premier league institutions of the country. The point to drive home is, a student now wants to pursue a management program not just in any school, but in the one that delivers value for his money and time; the one that gets him a career, not just a job. No doubt a staggering number of 2 lakh plus youth vie for a seat in the IIMs every year through CAT (Common Admission Test). So now the new equation for the business schools in India is 'Perform or Perish'.

STRENGTHS OF INDIAN MANAGEMENT EDUCATION

A number of favorable factors have helped in the rise of Indian Management Education from its humble beginnings in 1957 to what it is today. The biggest strength is the cost involved in turning out a graduate which is a fraction of what it costs outside India. Next is the adaptability that is ingrained as a culture in our systems as Indian management education benchmarked the curriculum and pedagogy from US business schools. Third is the availability of large pool of talented English speaking youths who are keen and enthusiastic to learn and do new things. India almost produces 30 per cent of the engineers the world requires, and this lays a sound foundation for the analytical and decision making skills of our managers as today most of the management students (50 per cent plus) come from engineering background. Comes next in the line, is the academic entrepreneurial streak among the prosperous Indians to invest in higher education and management education. Today Indian industry can boast of its managerial talent drawn mainly from the privately run business schools. This strength has resulted in yet another strength for private business schools, i.e. to modify the curriculum as per the market needs and enjoy the functional and operational freedom, both of which are not easily available to state funded or university programs. Most of the well run management programs have internships ranging from 8 to 14 weeks of duration where a student virtually becomes an employee of the organization he is interning in. This strengthens the industry – institute linkage which otherwise is highly essential. The IT skills Indians are known to possess have helped in furtherance of management education in the country. Last but not the least is the encouragement the Indian Management Education receives from the industry in terms of interface through assigning projects, placements, research grants, absorption of students on placements and participation in advisory boards, etc.

Indian Education System

Indian education system was known worldwide since ancient times with its universities at Nalanda, Vikramshila and Thakshashila attracting students from all over the world. The greatness further got enhanced with Kautilya's Arthshastra and Ramanujam's

Ganithashastra both of which, experts believe, have laid foundation for the modern economics and mathematics respectively. Heavy emphasis on mathematics, science and technology resulted in India producing around 2,50,000 engineers annually which is close to 30 per cent of the total engineers turned out world over. Mastery over quantitative concepts coupled with proficiency in English and IT proved to be a strength for Indians in the international job markets. Engineering education has now become a backbone for the management education and as a result, managers who are good in analytical and decision making skills are coming out of business schools. This fact is being acknowledged by the entrepreneurs and Chief Executive Officers (CEOs) as well. Government has also recognized the importance of education which is evident from the increasing budget allocation year after year. The aim is to make India a knowledge economy, and to bridge the demand and supply gap for talented manpower in both manufacturing and service sectors. Several leading MNCs look at education related measures as the way forward for India to emerge as a knowledge economy. Royce L Caplinger, Managing Director of Lockheed Martin says, "We are looking at India as a source of educated, trained and English speaking workforce. The continuing emphasis on education provides the necessary foundation" (Outlook, Mar 12, 2007). Indian education system in general and educated Indian youths in particular can look forward to many more Lockheed Martins in future.

Indian Management Education

Business education is a big business worth about $65 billion world over including corporate education of which management education alone is reported to be worth $22 billion, and growing at 10–12 per cent (SL Rao 2005). Indian management education is the latest academic discipline to arrive in the sub-continent having barely seen fifty odd springs. Yet it has made a mark for itself with over 2000 management institutes spread across the length and the breadth of the country turning out close to 1,00,000 graduates every year. The biggest plus point is the cost involved which is abysmal when compared with their western counterparts. No doubt the western world and the domestic markets are looking at Indian management institutes with bated breath to meet their ever increasing demand for talented manpower. 'Management' has become a buzzword and an education in it is expected to fetch a comfortable and well paid job. That is why all the bright and young Indians started weaning themselves away from central services, armed forces, state services or public sectors to get into corporate managerial stream through management education. This was partly because the initial impetus given by the government in establishing IIMs created a big brand value for themselves. Private operators did not lag behind and now there is a virtual scramble at the top, which augurs well for the Indian management education in general and for the graduating youth in particular.

Quality Manpower

Indian management faculty is known to have given to the world some of the best known brains in the academic fraternity who have done the country and the management discipline proud, CK Prahlad, Jagdish Seth, Sumantra Ghoshal and Raghuram Rajan, etc. to name a few. This is evident from the fact that our IIMs and IITs (Indian Institutes of Technology) figure in the top 100 best educational institutions in the world. Further evidence is available in the form of large percentages of Indian knowledge workers in American companies, educational institutions and scientific establishments to the extent of even heading some of them. Yet another fact is that year after year overseas companies flood the management institutes in India to pick up the best of the talent at mindblowing compensation packages. This by itself is a kind of tribute to the quality of manpower that some of our management institutes have produced though there are many issues yet to be addressed for improvement.

Government Policies

All India Council for Technical Education (AICTE) was established under an act of Parliament in 1987 as a statutory body like University Grants Commission (UGC) for planning, formulation of norms and standards, quality assurance, identifying priority areas for monitoring and evaluation, besides authorizing and approving new institutions and size of intakes and ensuring coordinated and integrated development of technical education in the country. Its purview included engineering, technology, architecture, pharmacy, hotel and catering technology and management. However the flip side of this is the extra focus of AICTE on engineering education with maximum of its staff having an engineering background. Management education had become incidental to AICTE. This cursory attention towards management education by the AICTE resulted in mushrooming growth of management institutes, mostly in the private sector, compromising the 'quality' issue. The council establishes All India Board for formulation of academic policies and plans. One such board, All India Board of Management Studies (AIB-MS) was constituted to look into the quality of management education which submitted its recommendations in 2003. But little has been done on this. AICTE has norms for recognizing management institutes, but subsequent to recognition the monitoring was not very satisfactory. This resulted in number of private institutes defaulting in the quality related systems. Many became teaching shops and reasons other than merit have started ruling the roost. For them, profit became a prime consideration where 'business education' got converted to 'business of education' setting aside all other norms. The AICTE has done precious little to discover these anomalies and penalize the offenders and impose order and discipline. However, it was the 'quality conscious' private operators who stayed out of AICTE fold and floated their own programs which were more than accepted by the industry. Other than the premier league institutes sponsored by the state it is these privately run non-AICTE management institutes that are creating a history in the management education scene in India. Government's support to them though implicit and unintended, has proved to be a boon for the management education in this country. The annual ranking surveys undertaken by the business press and the professional bodies have further boosted the 'quality performance' of business schools.

CHALLENGES BEFORE THE MANAGEMENT EDUCATION

Despite the exponential growth Indian management education has been able to achieve in the last half a century of its existence, the sector is facing serious challenges. Further growth of higher education and management education in this country, therefore depends upon understanding these challenges and addressing them expeditiously. Some of them are:

Scarcity of Faculty

Faculty forms the core of management education and their role is aptly described in our scriptures as, "*Aacharyat Padamadatte, Padam Sishya Swamedhaya, Padam Sahabrahmacharibhyaha, Sesham Kalakramenacha*", which means the teacher provides only one-fourth of the knowledge, while the student learns one-fourth on his own, the third portion comes from his peers and colleagues and the balance one-fourth knowledge a student picks up from the environment as the time passes on. This fits the management education like a hand in a glove. Though the teacher as per this 'shloka' is supposed to impart only one-fourth of the required knowledge, but it is he who facilitates the student to acquire the remaining three-fourths of the knowledge through various assignments, projects and case discussions, etc. Thus his role is very vital. Scarcity of faculty is a serious issue being faced by the management institutes not only in India but world over. With the number of schools that we have (2000 approx) at least 14,000 faculty members are required even at a modest scale of 7 per institute (AICTE norms). But the actual reported are meager 2000 indicating a glaring shortage of 12000. Even among the available, most of them are with the premier institutes leaving the next rung institutes with the less talented and non-Ph.D. teachers, while Ph.D. is an essential qualification for a management teacher as stipulated by AICTE. COSMODE in its study undertaken in early 2000 discovered that 70 per cent schools did not meet either of the above requirements. Availability of competent faculty is an important and serious concern for Indian business schools and will remain so in future too. With barely 4 per cent rate of growth of Ph.Ds. in management it would take enormously long time to produce the required number of Ph.D. faculty irrespective of the strategy that we adapt. Experts are of the opinion that a good business school requires a minimum of 25 members of faculty at least 4 in each of the functional areas of management. If this is taken as a norm then the shortage of faculty would be huge, requiring at least few thousands of Ph.Ds. to be churned out every year for the next 10 years or so assuming the number of business schools to remain static which is not likely. While that is not a simple task, institutes are initiating their own measures to overcome this problem like starting their own centers for management teachers to turn out Ph.D. faculty basically to meet its own internal requirements. In addition all premier management institutes (government and private) have started their own fellowship programs in management to get doctoral students by offering attractive emoluments. Then came the issue of academic faculty (core faculty) vis-à-vis the adjunct or visiting faculty from the industry as management discipline is highly application oriented and faculty without industry exposure, it was opined, would not do full justice to his teaching. A lot of debate had taken place on this in the last couple of decades and it was generally agreed to have 60 per cent core faculty and 40 per cent faculty with industry exposure. Some argued it should be 80–20. Despite all this most of the management institutes have not been adhering to this ratio and students are left at the receiving end.

Quality

The concept of quality in education has assumed significance hitherto unknown, all over the world. With the ever increasing demand for quality education and the stiff competition in the educational marketplace, the traditional state run education providers (excepting IIMs) are getting relegated down the chain by any one who delivers quality. Quality in general relates to distinguishing characteristics of a product or a service but the quality in education is what makes actual learning a great pleasure and a sheer joy. This joy in learning is ever changing and it is up to the teacher to gauge this and ensure that the student is wedded to learning. In the education process teaching occurs when one shows how to solve a problem and learning takes place when you know how to solve your problem. Improvement of both these processes is what constitutes quality management in education. Similarly features are those that differentiate one curriculum from the other while again the quality is the way these features are delivered to the student. Phenomenal rise in demand for management education appears to be diluting the 'quality' aspect of this professional program. Following quality related issues merit attention:

- Near or total absence of application orientation to management learning. Practicing managers rarely takeup to academics in our country, unlike in foreign countries.
- No meaningful tie-ups with industry or corporates (very few like Bharatidasan etc are exceptions).
- Little industry interface or attachment getting limited to hypothetical and repetitive projects for students.
- Research mostly getting restricted to academic topics with scanty relevance to industry.
- Most of the institutions engage part time faculty who have little or no involvement with the institution or the students.
- Teaching getting limited to contents in the textbooks by low paid faculty members.

- Infrastructural facilities in terms of libraries and computer labs are not satisfactory.
- Market oriented review of curriculum is not being undertaken on a regular basis.
- Students are found to be lacking in 'soft skills' by the companies and this proved to be a serious handicap.
- Faculty lack skills to deal with management of the business enterprise as a whole, and possess skills limited to their chosen area only.
- Admission of students without adequate screening.
- Lack of quality study material to suit Indian business environment.
- Lack of innovation in knowledge delivery mechanisms.
- Very high student to a teacher ratio.
- Lack of professionalism among the teachers and academic administrators.

Accreditation and Quality Assurance

Management education is seen as key to productivity and development, as it permeates the entire spectrum of human activity, as such, quality assumes critical importance. A study of COSMODE (1998) indicated that QA in higher business education is primarily the responsibility of regulatory agency and research organizations like:

- Accreditation by NAAC of UGC and NBA of AICTE is a rigorous assessment of quality.
- Ranking of business schools designed and pioneered by COSMODE, a research organization, provides continuous feedback on B-schools performance.

Association of Management Development Institutions in South Asia (AMDISA) a movement pioneered by Late Dharni P Sinha made concerted efforts to create quality consciousness among business schools in South Asia by benchmarking with the best in the world. They brought experts from AACSB, EFMD and conducted a workshop with about 100 Deans and Directors and developed a QA System unique to South Asian Countries called SAQS. Salient features are:

- Context and mission of the B-schools
- Contributions to society
- Academics and physical infrastructure
- Students and faculty
- Research, consultancy, training and development
- Programs, delivery and evaluation
- Executive education
- Leadership and personal development

However experts feel that there is a need for separate body for accrediting business schools in our country (SL Rao 2005).

COSMODE thus pioneered the ranking movement of Business schools in 1998 which sounded as a big alarm for them on the quality front. Subsequently, every year these rankings conducted by various professional organizations in close association with the business press are contributing a lot to the general improvements in the quality of most of the privately run business schools in the country. However there is still a need to have a 'change of mindset' in imparting quality management education in India.

Infrastructure Bottlenecks

Most of the management institutes in the country suffer from this weakness even till today despite their long standing in the field. Among the state run, all the IIMs are very sound in their infrastructure, but the university departments continue to suffer as most of them were started as extensions of their commerce departments. Private operators preferred to continue in the hired premises due to the high costs involved in making their permanent campuses.

Management education is a round the clock program where a student and faculty should be able to interact with each other at their free will as against the conventionally laid down official timings. The learning process involved demands such kind of infrastructure; as firstly all the schools have to be necessarily residential and academic infrastructure and ambience should be conducive to learning. Library and Internet facilities may be of top class, and in short the environment provided to the students and the faculty could ideally be conducive to draw out the best from them. Hardly 10 per cent (Dharni Sinha 2004) of the management institutes in the country can boast of this kind of infrastructure indicating the fact that the Indian management education field has still a long way to go in this aspect.

Competition Within

Management education in India used to be the sole prerogative of the elite when it was started in 1950s. The elitism of the program continued with the Indian Institutes of Management which have strict entry barriers with their CAT. However as the popularity of the program increased with the opening up of economy and the related reforms, the private sector got a boost and this resulted in opening up of scores of institutes all over the country. While the IIMs are maintaining their lead the university run departments at Delhi and Chandigarh are doing pretty well too. Private operators like SP Jain, XLRI and IBS have already inched their way to the top ten bracket and SP Jain, XLRI, and IMT even opened up overseas centers. IBS with its 16 branch network is the largest business school chain in the country and Indian Institute of Planning and Management (IIPM), Institute of Technology and Management (ITM), Institute for Management and Technology (IMT), Maharshi, Symbiosis, are some of the other multi branch networks of management schools operating in the country at a national level. Most of the university run departments of management and lower rung management schools cater to the regional or local requirements. All said and done, as the demand for this education is increasing, there is a corresponding rise in the competition. Indian School of Business

(ISB) started at Hyderabad in the year 2001 as a world class institution established with the help of Kelloggs, Wharton and London Business Schools has already carved a niche for itself by attracting students from overseas. The Great Lakes Institute of Management at Chennai started by academicians is also reported to be doing well. With a large number of private operators in the field showing keenness to climb the ranking ladders year after year, the existing stiff competition is likely to intensify further. This can be termed as a positive feature for Indian Management education.

Research and Consultancy

This has been a grey area in management education and continues to be so. It has been dealt as a separate chapter 6 in view of its growing importance for the faculty.

ISSUES IN MANAGEMENT EDUCATION: FUTURE PROSPECTS

It has been repeatedly observed that Indian business schools are positioning themselves more as placement agencies than as knowledge disseminators. This has led to increasing criticism that MBAs are overvalued. Some issues raised by the experts, viz., (Pesulima 1990), (Neelamkavil 1994), (Bicker Staff 1996) and (Yucelt 1998), are:

- MBA graduates are not adequately trained to meet global challenges.
- Faculty lack necessary business experience.
- Curriculum is mostly theoretical in nature.
- Over emphasis on quantitative subjects and less on social sciences.
- Inadequate industry – institute interface.
- Debatable employability of the graduates.
- Prohibitive cost of management education.
- Inadequate focus on research and consultancy.

- Lack of practical exposure to students.
- Schools giving false promises to aspiring students through misleading advertisements.
- Students passing out are not adequately trained for Non Governmental Organizations (NGOs), social sector, education sector or rural development.
- Inadequate attention towards values, ethics and Indian culture.

Angel Cabrea, President Thunderbird School of Global Management, Glendale, Arizona (2009), emphasizes the need for professionalizing the management education like medicine or law as a part of its reforming process. Towards this objective, more than two hundred business schools from around the world are reported to have endorsed the Principles of Responsible Management Education, a movement sponsored by the United Nations that promotes a view of business as contributing to a 'sustainable and global economy'. The teaching process must necessarily include diligent application of the specialized knowledge imparted, for resolving complex problems of social relevance. Business Schools could even consider adopting a professional code of conduct – a 'Hippocratic Oath of Business' as suggested by Rakesh Khurana and Nitin Nohria of HBS, to fulfill their obligations towards society. Thunderbird's experience of four years in adopting a 'Professional Oath of Honour' is reported to have delivered a renewed sense of pride in faculty and students with regard to the role management plays in social well being. While the world waits for a widely and universally acceptable professional code of conduct to be developed by World Economic Forum, business schools back home could take pride in having their own and follow it in true letter and spirit.

Industry and business press are performing the role of a watchdog and management institutes in the country have little or no choice but to rise up to the occasion by addressing these issues. India is soon going to need close to 1.3 lakh management graduates every year and the ball squarely rests on the side of the business schools to provide the required talent. Concerned with the not so satisfactory state of higher education in India Ministry of Commerce, Government of India, has recommended 100 per cent Foreign Direct Investment (FDI) in education and close to 700 foreign educational institutions are reported to be knocking at our doors to open shops here. Coupled with this, is the National Knowledge Commission's (NKC) report submitted to the Honorable Prime Minister recommending the establishment of 1500 universities in India and to increase the budgetary allocation for education. All this augurs well for the education field of which management education is a vital part. Management education in India has become so popular that very soon it is going to become a basic qualification for any job seeking individual. Such is the future poised for management education in India.

2

An Approach to HRM Practices in Business Schools

The term 'human resource' implies that people possess skills and capabilities that drive organizational performance along with other resources like money, material and machinery, and last but not the least is the information. All things being equal it is the 'people' who make the difference in the way an organization performs. Successful organizations are particularly adept at bringing together different kinds of people to achieve a common objective. This is the essence of Human Resource Management (HRM) in any organization, be it a business enterprise or an educational institution.

While people have always been central to organizations, today they have come to occupy centrestage, taking on a more central role in building the competitive advantage for the organization. Particularly in knowledge-based higher educational institutions such as management institutes, success largely depends upon 'people-centric know how'. This includes skills and abilities imbedded in an organization's members. In fact now the experts are of the opinion that an organization's success is based on establishing a set of 'core competencies'—the integrated knowledge sets within an organization that distinguish it from its competitors and deliver value to customers. Harvard Business School, for example, perfected the art of 'case method of teaching' which has been successfully benchmarked by IIM Ahmedabad and so many other business schools across the country. For example, IBS has gone one step further in having its own case development centres and it now claims as the single largest contributor of 'business cases for teaching' from India to ECCH (European Case Clearing House). Similarly there is a school of management at Warrick University in England dedicated to automobile industry which laps up all its MBAs. In India there is XLRI at Jamshedpur and TISS (Tata Institute of Social Sciences) at Mumbai which provide core HR professionals to the industry. Next is, the effective use of technology to impart net based education. UNext an online firm has established partnership with University of Chicago, Columbia, Stanford and INSEAD in order to provide a learning platform for an online education. U21 Global, based in Singapore has likewise forged partnership with several universities in Asia and Europe. Some Indian business schools like IIMs, XLRI, SP Jain and MDI, etc. have already taken initiative in providing net based education. Development of industry interaction is an evolutionary process. The main strengths of top class business schools like Kellogg, Wharton, Sloan, Stanford and Harvard are their strong relationship with industry through teaching, research, student placements, problem solving and case study preparation. The British Petroleum has set up their learning center at MIT which shows that as the competition increases, industry – B-school co-operation will go up. This international experience has served as a beacon light for the Indian business schools which are slowly but surely emerging as centres of excellence, establishing themselves by benchmarking certain good practices.

Management Institutes can achieve sustained competitive advantage through people if they are able to meet the following criteria: *(Resource based view model)*

- ***The resources must be of value:*** People become the source of competitive advantage when they improve the efficiency or effectiveness of the organization. Value is increased when faculty find ways to decrease costs, provide something unique to the customers, i.e. the students in our case, or some combination of the two. The faculties for various reasons in IIMs are a valued lot who in turn add value to their students and the whole process creates the 'brand value' they are enjoying today.

- ***The resources must be rare:*** Yet another method of making people as a competitive advantage is to make sure that their skills, knowledge and ability are not equally available to other management institutes. It may not be far from truth that most of the talented faculty get concentrated in premier institutes only, due to various reasons (generally compensation related) though other institutions have equally good faculty where they are more driven by 'passion' than by 'frills'.
- ***The resources must be difficult to imitate:*** Though this is more easily said than done, business schools must create their own unique culture making it difficult for others to imitate. Like the Indian School of Business at Hyderabad started a one year MBA program in India which others are trying to emulate now (IIM-A, XLRI, SP Jain and IBS) and it is yet to be seen how successful they would be.
- ***The resources must be optimized and organized:*** Faculty members may neither be underutilized nor overstretched, both of which are not desirable. Their talents could be pooled together and utilized optimally, if need be either through team assignments or through the use of information technology.
- ***The resources must be periodically evaluated:*** Periodic evaluation of knowledge possessed by faculty must be carried out for its relevance in the light of new areas emerging as a result of changes in market trends.

UNIQUE FEATURES OF MANAGEMENT EDUCATION

Management, in all its forms, is a critical activity of modern societies, deeply and inevitably shaping the livelihoods and lives of most people on earth. The best MBA programs and MBA teachers with real impact will make sure their students understand this extraordinary responsibility and opportunity.

– Prof Joe Badarraco

The management education sector is now a part of 'new economy' though it is barely a century old in the world and has hardly crossed the 50th milestone as far as the Indian subcontinent is concerned. This, education is 'unique' in its own way and unless this uniqueness is understood it may not be possible to develop sustainable HR strategies to manage the management faculty who constitute the core of the sector.

Management education is the most popular education all over the world, which according to some estimates is more than three times the number of law degrees, more than four times the number of engineering degrees and more than seven times the number of medical degrees. Situation is no different in India too as MBA Program at PG (Postgraduate) level is the most popular choice among the graduating youth of this country, with engineering still retaining its top position as far as undergraduate courses are concerned. The conceptual and analytical skills that are honed, and the wisdom that is drilled into management education, only go to make an individual endowed with the most powerful business tools ready to take on the corporate wars. Some of the unique features of management education from the point of view of faculty and students are summarized and presented below:

Unique Features: Faculty Perceptions

- Knowledge and skills need continuous updating
- Highly demanding in terms of quality output of students

- People and knowledge intensive sector
- Requires adequate business related and cross-functional knowledge
- Research and publication are essential attributes
- Need to master the art of interactive teaching
- Intensive competition among the top institutes
- No organized HR practices in place
- Industry interface is essential
- Need to possess sound soft skills
- Expected to meet high expectations of students (Value for Money – VFM) in terms of knowledge delivery and subsequent placements.
- Contribute to brand and image building of the institute

Unique Features: Student Perceptions

- High application orientation
- Involves continuous study and evaluation
- Integrated approach to business through all functional disciplines
- Generally relative grading system is resorted to
- Personality development oriented
- Highly profession oriented
- Teamwork involved (cases, projects and assignments)
- Calls for Interactive mode of learning through questioning
- Heavy emphasis on self-learning
- High assignment intensive
- Heavy emphasis on soft skills
- Demands plenty of peer group interaction and learning from each other
- Case study and project intensive
- Close industry involvement through projects
- Market oriented curriculum

- Includes entrepreneurial skills too among various other skills like conceptual, analytical, decision making, etc.
- Emphasis on result-oriented activities
- Commercial sense and business bottom line orientation

CONCEPT OF A MANAGEMENT TEACHER

Before the concept of a management teacher is discussed it is pertinent to take a relook at the concept of a teacher itself.

Teacher is 'a person who teaches or educates someone and whose accountability does not end with the academic performance of the students. He is one who leaves his foot prints behind.' More often than not teaching at best gets limited to imparting subject knowledge, speaking in its conventional sense, which in a way does not do justice to the term 'education' which is defined as 'the understanding and interpretation of knowledge. It is the process of transmission of accumulated knowledge and imparting of quality of mind and character. In general it is the overall development of all round personality of an individual'. Thus a teacher has a dual responsibility, one to teach the student and the next, to develop the personality of the student, strangely, attention is rarely paid to the latter.

In the light of above mentioned explanations, the concept of management teacher has to be based on the role he is expected to play to meet the unique requirements of management education discussed already. In short the concept can be explained as "Management Teacher is the one who apart from imparting subject knowledge teaches the basics of application of the knowledge so imparted, making a concerted effort to make a manager and a good human being out of an ordinary and simple individual."

As explained above, teachers particularly management teachers are involved in acquiring, creating and disseminating knowledge. Hence it is logical to categorize them as knowledge workers. Harringan and Dalmiya define knowledge workers as 'key employees who create value added areas'. Peter Drucker who coined this term defines knowledge workers as 'high level employees who apply their theoretical and analytical knowledge acquired through formal education, to developing new products and services'. He pointed out that knowledge workers have high mobility and their own means of production which is their knowledge and ideas. In the emergent knowledge based economy, employers' need for knowledge workers will be more than workers' need for employers. Now a teacher assumes the role of a knowledge worker as he passes through the stages of merely telling (mediocre teacher), explaining (good teacher), demonstrating (superior teacher) and finally as a great teacher he inspires the students. The knowledge he possesses, which he constantly keeps on upgrading, becomes the intellectual property of the institution. These knowledge workers and their knowledge is going to command the market premium. The concept of knowledge worker which raised a new school of thought necessitating a new set of HR practices to manage him, as he has special needs and requires a particular environment to work effectively and productively. This school of thought advocates that a preferential treatment is essential to management faculty in pay and perks. This is more so in the light of the fact that the students taught and trained by these very faculty members command much higher salaries when they complete the program and join the companies.

Edwards Deming W (1900–1993) and Reuven Feurstein have been pioneers in the fields of management and education. Deming introduced a new paradigm for management while Feurstein heralded a new paradigm for learning. As we apply the concept of total quality of Deming to education it is the education of the student that is treated as the product and not the student himself. Hence labeling teachers as knowledge workers is more than justified as both input and output is knowledge in their case. Even according to Davenport's classification of knowledge workers as knowledge creators and knowledge users fits the role of teachers as they create knowledge through research and use it or disseminate it to educate students.

Management teacher is not only a knowledge disseminator but also needs to be a creator as knowledge is the basis for his survival. Therefore he builds his knowledge assiduously. The knowledge system of the management faculty consists of two independent subsystems of 'delivery' and 'gestation'. Through delivery he strives to utilize his ready to use competencies in his day-to-day work. And through gestation he works towards learning, practicing and assimilating knowledge of futuristic developments in management science. Gestation is the only safeguard and insurance in an industry where the pace of technological advancements is rather high.

CHARACTERISTICS OF MANAGEMENT TEACHERS AS KNOWLEDGE WORKERS

Keeping the unique features of management education in view, it is relevant to examine certain typical characteristics of management teachers as knowledge workers which are enumerated below:

- Management teachers invest substantial time, effort and resources to acquire relevant knowledge and expertise in the chosen area of discipline.
- They look forward to use their existing knowledge and acquire new knowledge on a continuous basis so as to survive and grow in an industry where old knowledge becomes obsolete very fast.
- They tend to be highly analytical and hence they expect rationale for every activity. They also expect to be involved in defining and planning every organizational change affecting them and the organization.
- They tend to be high achievers and hence they expect periodical and tangible feedback and recognition for performance. Since reward system is perceived as a part of the feedback system, linking performance with reward

and expecting equity in reward become very important for them.

- They are willing to work on new assignments to improve their learning.
- Management faculty as knowledge workers generally tend to be more committed to their profession than to the organization they are working for.
- They value autonomy, professionalism and innovativeness.
- Due to large gaps existing in demand and supply situation, they are able to move from their present organization to new organization.

Special

While the above characteristics are general in nature, more specific attributes of a management faculty, which he needs to possess, to be a successful knowledge worker are listed below. They could also be termed as Key Performance Indicators (KPIs) for faculty members.

- Acquisition of knowledge in the relevant area and continuous updating of the same. Creation of new knowledge through research
- Sound business awareness and commercial sense
- Cross-functional knowledge and integrated approach to business
- Being a 'Role model', for students
- Play an active role in curriculum design, review and pedagogy
- Involve in personality development of students
- Seek feedback from students and the management
- Work for institutional image building
- Be a member of professional bodies, participate in meets, and contribute to professional publications
- Resort to innovative methods of course delivery, and examinations, etc.

- Maintain continuous industry interface through consultancy and projects to update himself with relevant application techniques of the theoretical concepts.
- Be an active and vibrant part of the institution.
- Work to instill a sense of entrepreneurship in the students.

HR STRATEGIES FOR MANAGING 'MANAGEMENT TEACHERS'

Management Education is a knowledge intensive sector. As such there is a dire need to have the right HR strategies in place to attract, develop, nurture, compensate, motivate, assess and retain the knowledge workers (faculty). In the following paragraphs, a brief discussion is made on some of these strategies, as an approach to a more detailed discussion of the same in the subsequent chapters.

Before taking up the actual discussion it is relevant to recall the high calling of management education in present recession and scam ridden business scenario. Rakesh Khurana and Scott Snook of HBS (2009) offer a simple set of suggestions to business school faculty in this regard.

- ***Be honest and truthful:*** There is a need to understand the value of truth over sophistry.
- ***Avoid conflicts of interest:*** Faculty enjoys a great deal of academic freedom which should not be misused to meet personal ends.
- ***Never lose the sense of humility:*** New discoveries and interpretations should result in one becoming more humble than before in stating what one knows.
- ***Being realistic about the fruits of labour:*** Faculty should necessarily be concerned about the impact their teaching has on the society, and not to be insensitive to it.

The authors caution the business schools not to exploit the academic freedom and the autonomy to self-regulate themselves, and continue to work in the best interests of the society, so as not to lose the privilege.

Attracting Talent

It has been estimated that there is a need for almost 12,000 trained faculty in management if all schools, both recognized and otherwise, are to meet the minimum norms. This is without counting the large number of existing faculty (2000 of them) who must be trained in teaching management students, because most come to management classrooms, with no other background except in their own subject and no exposure as to how they must tailor their teaching to fit management teaching. MBA is recognized as a professional education in this country. Therefore there is an expectation that institutes awarding Postgraduate Diploma in Management or MBA must have academic faculty along with those who are successful practicing managers in the field. While there is a consensus to have a mixed profile of the faculty there is a strong disagreement among the business schools about the ratio of core academic faculty to the visiting faculty. In a workshop held at one of the management institutes most Deans of business schools were of the opinion that at least 60 per cent of the core courses should be taught by academic faculty having Ph.D., M.Phil. or Fellowship qualifications. Some felt that 80–20 ratio would be ideal and many divergent views were also expressed. In the South Asian Management Colloquium held in Maldives participated by Deans of business schools, business leaders and policy administrators from 7 South Asian Countries concluded that at least 10 core academic faculty will do justice to the management education in business schools. However in general, an agreement was arrived at, on involving academic faculty for core courses and visiting faculty or the industry/professional faculty to teach elective courses Strategies suggested to be adopted to attract faculty are:

- One private university for instance has a faculty referral program wherein an existing faculty can refer a new faculty and earn a handsome incentive after six months (50 per cent) and one year service of the new faculty (balance 50 per cent).

- IIMs and other premier institutes run fellowship programs and on completion of the same the trainees are absorbed as faculty.
- Management institutes spot the talent in seminars/ conferences among delegates hailing from academic/ industry backgrounds.
- Yet another private university runs an exclusive institute for management teachers where MBAs with some work experience are taken, put through a three year program leading to the award of Ph.D. and then absorbed as faculty, to meet its own internal requirements.
- Existing faculty in some management institutes inspire and motivate students to take up management teaching as a profession. University run departments score on this over the others.
- Some institutes like Jamnalal Bajaj Institute of Management (Department of Management Education in Bombay University) mostly depend on guest faculty from the industry drawing from the advantage of being located amidst business district of Mumbai. Indian School of Business at Hyderabad has more visiting faculty from the universities abroad, than their own permanent faculty.
- By and large most of the institutes go for open advertisement to seek new talent.

Development of Management Teachers

Unlike in the IT industry where the rate of obsolescence of technology is very high, management education is more market-driven hence development of faculty becomes highly relevant. Consequently continuous upgradation of knowledge and skills assumes critical significance. Providing opportunities for learning comes under the purview of the managements, which value growth and development of its faculty. As a result, continuous learning becomes an essential operational feature in business schools. Strategies that could be considered in this aspect are:

- Orientation or Induction training to faculty (compulsory) before taking up actual classes in management. Students undergoing Fellowship Programs in premier institutes and Research Scholars of, IIMT necessarily undergo this training.
- Number of premier business schools in the country (IIMs, IBS, XLRI etc.) run Faculty Development Programs (FDPs) mostly during summers while there is a lull in the campuses of other institutes on the academic front.
- Tendency to burden the faculty with teaching load is detrimental to self-development, hence institutions may have their own norms ranging from 6 hours to 8 hours (maximum). IBS has just ≠ 7½ hours of teaching load per week (6 sessions of 1 hour and 15 minutes duration each) that is to say, the management has to provide the teacher with sufficient time to prepare adequately for his teaching and also to undertake self-developmental activities like research and publications, institution building, etc. Too much of teaching load may in some cases result in a teacher using the same content year after year without significant value addition which is detrimental specially for management education as the same is highly market/ industry oriented. Ideal load would be, just 4 sessions of 1 hour 30 minutes duration each, per week.
- Training in maintaining continuous industry interface with summer projects, assignments, organizing joint events like seminars and conferences, etc. Nirma Institute of Management (NIM) Ahmedabad for instance has been conducting International Conferences in Management (NICOM) every year for the last ten years.
- Encouraging research and publication culture including case writing by having required platforms. All the premier

institutes run their journals. ICFAI University Press here again scores over the rest with host of developmental facilities in this regard.

- Provision of excellent libraries (including physical and online) is a very essential developmental facility in any management institute.
- Incentive oriented development facilities for research, publication, case writing, handling extra teaching assignments, projects generation and supervision, etc. are in vogue in number of business schools.
- Faculty is encouraged to take up Executive/Management Development Programs (EDP and MDP) and consultancy assignments which are professionally advancing, stimulating apart from being highly remunerative. All IIMs, ISB, XLRI, etc. have their calendars full for the entire year, with these programs.

Development related activities are closely linked to HRM aspects of management institutes which form the core of our book. Training a faculty in acquiring a particular skill is generally short-term oriented while providing developmental facilities help in achieving long-term objectives as they result in holistic development of faculty's personality. Hence development of faculty is highly essential.

Compensation

No matter what, besides other factors money still continues to be the single largest motivating and retention factor for any employee, more so for a knowledge worker like management faculty. Intense competition fueled by mushrooming growth of business schools created a dearth for quality faculty and hence the demand for talent and value for it in terms of financial packages. Management faculty is a highly networked group interacting with each other in various seminars and conferences. Consequently they become aware of salaries, perks and other facilities offered to peers in other institutions. That's how the job hopping process starts. They not only want higher rewards but are equally conscious of equity. This makes the job of managing the compensation system not only complex but also quite challenging. There are basically two types of compensation structures under the government fold. One is AICTE pay scales structure and the other is UGC pay scales both which have been recently revised to the advantage of faculty. Most of the state run or even some top rung private business schools operate on AICTE pay scale structure (IIMs and IBS etc.) while few others pay as per UGC norms, which are comparable. Premier league private schools like XLRI, SP Jain, etc. have their own norms which are better than either AICTE or UGC scales. Compensation could be cited as one of the main reasons for fall in the quality in Indian education system in general and in management education in particular. Traditionally or historically, unfortunately teaching as a profession in our country is not much valued. This is evident from the fact that in India academic faculty receives far less salary than fresh MBAs who join companies. Therefore there is a pull towards job market in the industry and push away from the academics. The situation in most of the lower rung private schools is pathetic on the compensation front.

IIMs have relatively less number of 'compensation' issues compared to their counterparts as the faculty gets handsomely rewarded through consultancy and EEP/EDP and MDP etc. (Executive Education Program – EEP). Institutions like Institute of Management Technology (IMT) and IBS either have liberal pay scales or pay adequate incentives to the faculty in proportion to their extra efforts in any field of interest to the organization. Icfai University goes to the extent of offering free education to the children of their employees who have put in five years of service. By and large it is observed that there is a general dissatisfaction among the faculty about the compensation they receive for their efforts, as the salary structures in education sector have not been keeping pace with the changing living standards unlike the corporate sector.

Performance Management

Performance management basically constitutes provision of a conducive working environment and ample growth avenues for the people to come out with their best foot forward in terms of output. It should ideally incorporate both developmental and reward-oriented objectives with a sound appraisal or assessment system in place. Any compromises in the laid down periodicity of appraisals will be counter productive, in a business school which it can ill afford.

Retention and Separation

Lateral move of business school faculty is as common as in case of corporate executives. This is more prevalent among the private sector business schools with the doctoral and otherwise skilled faculty who are generally more in demand. The situation gets further aggravated due to their acute shortage and 'poaching' tactics of rival business schools. Hence sound retention strategies are of critical importance in business schools. Equally vital is the 'happy separation' process as there are instances when the faculty gets back to their former institutions for various reasons.

ISSUES AND CHALLENGES

Indian Management education today is grappling with many a challenge in so far as they relate to human resource management. They could hinge around the expectations of both students and faculty from the institutions, ensuring a proper teamwork to deliver wholesome and integrated knowledge to the student, and to create a informal work environment in a culture of openness and transparency with a view to strike a perfect balance in work and family life. The whole idea is to make sure that the faculty gives his best and the student receives nothing less than the best, as value for his money.

Expectations of Management Teachers

Teachers by and large, are simple souls and so are their expectations. Though simple, management faculty is quite assertive and sensitive about their expectations, like any other knowledge worker. Briefly some of these expectations as observed by the author during the course of research and practical experience are summarized and presented below:

- Satisfying compensation and rewards for hard work
- Conducive working environment through sound infrastructural facilities
- Guaranteed self-esteem
- Self-development and career progression facilities
- Equality and fair play
- Enthusiastic and responsive set of students to teach
- Facilities and encouragement for creativity and innovation.
- Value adding experience through research and training
- Psychologically fulfilling time (feeling of having done something worthwhile)
- Recognition and appreciation of quality work

Expectations of Students

Management program is a professional and career oriented program, and hence is a very popular choice among the graduating youth of the country. By all counts put together, close to a million young aspirants appear for admissions tests in various management schools of the country. The seats in IIMs and other premier institutions are eagerly contested for. There is a very good reason why the MBA degree is so popular. Its interdisciplinary approach, the job potential and guarantee for a comfortable and well paid career and of course the glamour that is attached to it, all put together draw the students to business schools. On the learning side, the program addresses key concepts, hones skills and provides relevant tools packing in all, the whole lot of wisdom. With this background, the expectations of the students are enumerated below:

- Sound entry barriers to ensure quality intake
- Quality teaching and pedagogy
- Leveraging on the brand value of the school
- Sound infrastructural arrangements to facilitate learning process, in terms of libraries, Internet, and computing facilities and technically sound classrooms
- Value for money as the fee charged in most of the private business schools is rather high
- Guaranteed placement on completion of the program
- Facilities for peer group interaction and learning
- Sound alumni network
- Industry interface through projects and special assignments
- Facilities to showcase latent talents
- Fair and unbiased evaluation systems
- Well-organized residential campus in terms of good hostels, messes, cafeterias, and other recreational facilities
- Counseling facilities for career progression and personal problems
- Soft skills for personality development
- 'Earn while you learn' programs
- Student exchange programs with foreign universities, if any

Working in Teams

Intellectuals or knowledge workers though may not be averse to working in teams but they are not comfortable either. This is quite apparent in high research oriented faculty who generally would like to confine themselves to books and the computer. This is not a very conducive work culture of a management institute as the above listed expectations of a student can only be met when management faculty work as a team. Moreover, business knowledge is the sum of all functional disciplines taught by individual faculty members. Every faculty is also expected to possess cross-functional knowledge in addition to his own while discussing cases and application techniques. That calls for a close interaction with the colleagues of other disciplines too. This harmony among the faculty can be achieved through simple measures like having mid morning tea together as they do in MDI in Gurgaon, XLRI in Jamshedpur or celebrate festivals or successes together through parties, etc. Getting the faculty together to organize a seminar or a conference is the single most unifying and professionally satisfying gesture on the part of the leader/management. Yet another area is to assign projects by forming cross-functional teams or asking them to undertake executive education programs and consultancy assignments, etc. Rotation of faculty in key assignments is yet another stimulating activity to facilitate teamwork. The entire team should be rewarded equally in case of good work, and same should be the case for reproof too.

Work Life Balance

Management teachers enjoy being with their books and computers to the point of being highly addictive. While working on projects, consultancy assignments or research, they tend to lose track of time by putting in long hours of work. Another peculiar aspect of management programs is its residential nature both for students and teachers in the same campus. This makes the faculty accessible to students on a round the clock basis, as discussions on cases and projects carry on till late hours and even beyond. This is yet another expectation of the students specially of premier institutes to seek faculty guidance on demand, irrespective of the time and day. Most of the issues are being addressed through email or telephone, still personal touch is what students crave for and no worthwhile institution can afford to disregard this vital expectation of the students. Added to this is the institutional pressures on research (pre- and post-doctoral), publications and paper presentations, etc. Many institutes value 'student feedback' on faculty as an important tool for assessing the performance of the faculty. Strangely some organizations tend to attach more value for longer hours of working than the actual output or its quality. Over a period of time the process of working long hours disturbs the balance between work and non-work life and good management teachers tend to experience burn out.

Any working person is expected to perform many roles related to work and domestic (non-work) life. However, since good management teachers tend to spend much time on work related activities all the other roles tend to become unimportant and at times even irrelevant to them, so much so the personal identity often merges with the role identity. For example, if a faculty is a good organizer, he repeatedly gets the responsibility of organizing seminars and conferences both at national and international levels. If he is also good intellectually, then a lot more is expected from him on this front. As knowledge workers, they tend to enjoy the attention and the importance they get. Professionals operating at self-actualization level tend to define their self-concept in terms of their work and hence they may not feel bad when work becomes all encompassing and all consuming. Besides work becomes instrumental in getting tangible rewards from the organization. Hence consciously or sub-consciously, they 'exchange their free time and domestic life roles for organizational performance and tangible rewards associated with them'. However the vacuum due to lack of non-work life activities sooner or later leads to emptiness within and annoyance with the organization. There would be a stage when frustration sets in and this results either in lateral movements of the faculty within the business schools as it happens generally or it may even wean away a faculty permanently from the academics as it happened in case of one young faculty at one of the IIMs (Business World Oct 03, 2005 P. 66). Business schools must be proactive in instituting correctional mechanisms through either sabbaticals, faculty exchange programs or even providing industry exposure through attachments, etc. Any hardworking individual would enjoy these changes and refresh himself to give his best to the organization all over again, and neither business schools nor its committed faculty is any exception to this rule.

DESIGNING A COMPELLING CULTURE

Management faculty members are highly competitive and ambitious as knowledge workers and they thrive in an environment that encourages high performance. In this field, the students and their parents are the customers and high customer orientation like in any other business enterprise, is the only key for survival. A faculty member needs to be in touch with the industry on a continuous basis to assess the degree of utility of his product—the student—and to assess the adequacy of the course curriculum. Contact with the student on 24×7 basis is highly essential and an occasional touch with the parents will only boost the institutional image. To deliver high quality of service to all the above mentioned customers, the faculty needs an atmosphere of functional freedom to take decisions as deemed fit. To take these decisions it is necessary that they should be empowered to act as authorized representatives of the schools they work for. Most of the business schools have provided for a flattened hierarchy with just 2 or 3 levels as a measure of this empowerment. In fact Dean or Director appointments in some schools are on a rotation basis. Since the work is knowledge intensive and highly result oriented, factory like rigour would be detrimental and is normally frowned upon by the faculty. Most of the university departments and business schools having well laid out campuses permit flexi-time for their faculty. In short, an organizational culture that promotes harmony, freedom of thought, expression and action, at the same time result oriented and which ensures rewards and recognition is what is called for in a 'business school'.

SKILL UPGRADATION

Institutions committed to the cause of management education must make an effort to develop a more structured support to the new faculty that includes student mentoring and their individual professional development as teachers. The induction training is to be designed with an objective to provide an orientation to the new faculty members entering the system. The orientation should ideally revolve round the institutes' education philosophy, and the urgent need to break the traditional 'chalk and talk monologue' and foster a participative learning environment. The focus may be on the student and his learning and not on the teacher and his teaching. This is the hallmark of the management faculty, to start with. Unless a faculty embarks on this journey first, he/she is not going to go very far in business school academics.

Next is the aspect of 'learning while teaching'. A faculty should not have any inhibitions in sitting in the classes of his senior colleagues alongside students and learn the tricks of the trade or master the nuances of the fine art of teaching. Quality teaching takes place only when there is a joy of learning. A teacher can convert teaching into a fine creative craft and make learning an exciting experience for the students. For this a teacher must first learn to unlearn, and constantly search to innovate and bring creative teaching methodologies to the classroom.

Most of the above training takes place in the first two years of a management teacher's service and by their third year most teachers are comfortable with the routine of their job and are ready to go deeper into subject areas. They would also be ready to master the content and learn new ways to present it. This is how the teachers having been given adequate preparation time get used to the complexities of management teaching so that they can deliver quality teaching.

"Expanding the repertoire" is something all management faculty need to undertake throughout their careers. It is a kind of professional responsibility without which, faculty falls into predictable patterns that fail to excite students about learning, as they possess the uncanny skill of identifying the 'routine types' quickly—the kind who use the same set of slides year after year, for batch after batch.

Certain measures which premier institutes like IIMs, IBS, MDI and SP Jain, XLRI, XIMB and some universities and autonomous institutions adopt to upgrade skills among their faculty are listed below:

- Induction/orientation program for every incoming faculty.
- Mentoring programs for the first time faculty.
- Faculty Development Programs (FDPs) on regular basis (quarterly/half yearly/yearly).
- Encouragement to take up pre- or post-doctoral research work through incentives.
- Encouragement to take up self-development activities like publication of articles, and editing magazines and journals.
- Encouragement to present papers in regional/national/international seminars including organizing them at institution level.
- Sending faculty to universities abroad on 'faculty exchange' programs.

3
The Road Traversed

To travel hopefully is a better thing than to arrive, and the true success is to labour.

– R.L. Stevenson (El Dorado 1881)

Though there is not much literature available nor much research undertaken on HRM issues in management institutes but an abundant research was carried out on management education as such. This research in one way or the other did highlight the HRM issues of management institutes in the form of quality of their products. Business schools are pivotal in developing managerial manpower, but exclusive focus or overemphasis on teaching makes them akin to any other centre of learning and is not likely to advance management education per se as an academic discipline. Thus there is a dire need to lay stress on research and application of acquired knowledge by the faculty. Though the literature on HR processes is scanty in business schools or institutions of higher learning, a pioneering effort was made in this direction by two researchers way back in the year 1995 itself.

David Warner and Elaine Crosthwaite in their edited version of the book *Human Resource Management in Higher and Further Education* (SRHE: The Society for Research into Higher Education & Open University Press 1995) emphasized the following:

- The HR professional must operate at top level. The HR strategy must form part of overall organizational strategy (Elizabeth Lanchberry).
- A diverse workforce is essential to contribute a valuable range of skills and abilities (Rebecca Nestor).

- The institutions must encourage life long learning by mentoring and coaching (Jennifer Tann).
- The educational environment does not differ significantly from the commercial world in so far as a large proportion of its success will come from the contributions of a well-motivated workforce bound together by effective communication (Jo Andrews).
- Performance Management is not satisfactory to maintain achievements of the past or to enable staff to improve their future performance (David Bright and Bill Williamson).
- The advantage of using executive recruiters to assist with academic appointments are numerous (Diana Ellis).

Further a brief review of the literature available on management education indicates the relevance of the following issues which are related to HRM either directly or indirectly.

A three-point agenda for improving management education was proposed by McFarland (1960) which says that the faculty must redefine their own academic image, the departments must cast off shackles of an undistinguished past and orient themselves genuinely towards scientific research. An MIT study showed that significant attitude changes had taken place in students after the advent of management education. Another study by Luthans Walker and Hodgetts (1969) concluded that a college degree is a self-validating criterion for success. Japanese domination in the global economy led to review the current management education and its relevance due to its high profit orientation for business. The quality thus suffered a setback which was highlighted by Carnegie foundation study of 1959. The study indicated the poor quality of faculty, business education lacking, a clear sense of mission and goals and low academic standards. Rehder (1982) indicated the resistance of the management for change and predicted the setting up of corporate universities which eventually came true. In 1982 AACSB and EFMD in their study titled "Managers for XXI Century" recommended that management education should be more holistic in character, integrating number of functional fields and involving a 'continuum of learning' with self-teaching. Two more studies by Wexley and Baldwin in 1986 and by Keys and Wolfe in 1988 emphasized the need for comprehensive approach to management development as enhanced accountability for quality, increased use of experiential techniques and educational technology and a recognition of the need for life long learning. Handy Report and Constable and Mc Cormick Report of UK suggested the critical need for appropriate measures to overcome the shortage of high quality faculty to ensure both quality and quantity of future supply of executives which was also supported by Osbaldeston and Barham (1989). These reports emphasized that training is a strategic weapon. Storey and Sisson (1990) stressed that faculty needs to develop new skills that will help them to meet the changing demands of the industry. A series of criticisms about the operation of business schools that appeared in 1993 (Hasan, Raelin) reported that the faculty preferred to teach what was deemed fit rather than what the companies actually wanted. These criticisms resulted in a series of changes with AACSB adopting a new accreditation process. Then came globalization which made management schools change their outlook, without which they could not have survived. It was almost certain that institutions lacking a vigorous, systematic and coherent strategy for internationalization of the curricula would put all concerned at a serious disadvantage. Global companies recognize the need to develop leaders who are equally comfortable and effective working anywhere in the world (Miller 1998). Howe and Martia (1998) indicated that best practices cannot easily be transferred across the globe. One of the major problems that they identified was that of finding an internationalization strategy that accommodates the interests of western business schools as well as those of the host countries. Management education and management practices are converging (Martin & Butler 2000).

Boyatzis and Renio (1989) undertook exhaustive research on the impact of MBA education by comparing MBA applicants and graduates and found higher self-evaluation among MBA graduates in six managerial skills indicating definitive advantages gained from MBA studies. The researches undertaken by Pesulima (1990) Neelamkavil (1994), Bickerstaffe (1996) and Yuselt (1998) indicated the shortage of faculty and their lack of necessary business experience among various other things. Epsey and Batchelor (1987) had concluded that management graduates improve a company's effectiveness, both the short and the long term. This was further corroborated by Kane (1993), Bale and McCulloch (1993), Roth (1990), Baruch and Leerning (1996), Sheridan (1993) and Shipper (1999) identified the need for MBA curriculum to keep pace with changing business needs. This in turn requires the faculty to update their knowledge and skills. Eberhardt's (1997) research proved that 22 per cent HR managers do not want to recruit MBA graduates for their lack of leadership skills which in a way is a reflection of quality of faculty and the pedagogy.

However, the same research indicated that consultancy firms prefer MBAs for their analytical skills. This was confirmed in various other researches of Porter (1997), Quacquarelli (1998) and Kretovics (1999). Porter and Mc Kibbin (1988) commissioned by AACSB opined that business schools were not doing enough to develop 'soft skills' among their graduates, and they recommended inclusion of public speaking, conflict resolution, negotiation, and teamwork techniques in the curriculum, in addition to company internship for practical application of theoretical concepts learnt. Thus there is a strong need for the faculty to develop these skills among themselves in the first place. AMDISA Workshop on Reinventing Management Education highlighted the necessity for National Centre for management teacher development and felt the need for advancement of management knowledge, appropriate teaching skills and industry know-how. Various business schools surveys emphasize on faculty, intellectual capital and program delivery, as vital parameters for rankings. This in turn calls for a well-qualified and talented faculty. Globalization and technological advancement have propelled the quality aspects of management education in the overall development of economic and social enterprise. There have been several attempts to transfer business model of Total Quality Management (TQM) to higher education. RW Harris (1994) indicated that the TQM was being adopted by number of universities which was further authenticated by Peter Hosie in 1995. A study by Priscilla Chadwick (1916) indicated that as universities become increasingly accountable for the quality of their teaching and learning, alongside the quality of their research and academics, they need to improve their understanding of educational process. The traditional response to this has been to provide staff development courses for academics to improve their teaching skills. He argued that universities additionally need to strengthen the more strategic role of educational development working with academics across the institution to enhance academic quality in terms of cross discipline knowledge. Yin Cheong Cheng and Wai Ming Tam (1997) indicated that Quality Assurance often fails in higher education systems. They suggested seven models of quality in education. The goals and specification model; the resources input model; the process model, the satisfaction model, the legitimacy model, the absence of problem model and the organizational learning model. They concluded that these models can form a comprehensive framework for understanding and conceptualizing the quality in education from different perspectives and facilitating development of management strategies for achieving it. A case study by Linga Murthy N and Sita Vanka on HRM of Higher Education Institutions in India—A Study of Kakatiya University by applying Guest Model (1989)—highlighted the necessity of an integrated approach and application of professional management principles in HRM of higher educational institutions. Yet another case study titled "Leveraging Human Potential through HRM Strategy: A Case Study of Jawaharlal Nehru Technological University" (JNTU-2002) by Venkatrami Reddy Y emphasized on high performance standards with commitment to excel through judicious and prudent use of resources.

One of the major elements that helped management education in US and UK was the accreditation process which unfortunately was not very stringent in our country, leaving a lot to be desired in furtherance of management education. Back home Nanda Committee was the first committee (1981) that reviewed the working of three IIMs at Ahmedabad, Kolkata and Bangalore who opined that management education should be research based, utility based, and that the institutes must be self-reliant with minimal or nil governmental control. This again drives the point home about the quality of the faculty. The Kurien Committee (1991) report highlights the need for increased emphasis on the development of relevant teaching materials and research. The committee felt that appropriate policies and rewards should be initiated to strengthen this aspect of IIMs functioning. Subsequent to this report IIMs reoriented their operations then followed the Ishwar Dayal Committee which submitted its report in 2001 but the regulatory body could not initiate any new measures for faculty development or development of teaching materials.

Finally, in 2003 AICTE appointed 'The Management Education Review Committee' to come up with a policy and action plan for the development of management education in India in the context of our current national requirements and trends. One of the highlights of committee's report is the mention of critical and severe shortage of faculty in management education. All the above mentioned committees have however indicated that management education in India suffers from the following limitations. They are:

- Shortage of faculty and quality of faculty
- Promotion and neglect of research culture
- Little attention towards preparation of course material
- Poor libraries and infrastructure facilities
- Inadequate or lack of institution-industry interface
- Lack of faculty development facilities

Yet another issue prevalent in the business schools across the globe today is the lack or limited focus on ethics and Corporate

Social Responsibility (CSR) in the curricula. Late Sumantra Ghoshal of London Business School (LBS) in his paper titled 'Bad Management Theories are Destroying Good Management Practices' (Journal of Academy of Management Learning & Education Mar 2009) highlighted the following:

- Business School faculty need to own up to their own role in creating Enrons.
- Lack of impact of management research on management practice and the lack of effectiveness of management education for business performance of students.
- By propagating ideologically inspired amoral theories business schools have actively freed their students from any sense of moral responsibility.
- Tendency to treat business studies as 'science' denying the places for moral and ethical considerations in theories and consequently in prescriptions for management practices.
- It is not proper to pretend that the methods of the physical sciences can be freely applied to business education too because such pretension ignores the fundamental difference between the two disciplines.
- Management faculty as 'social scientists' carry an even greater social and moral responsibility than those who work in the physical sciences because if they hide ideology in the pretence of science, they can cause much more harm.
- A tokenism of adding a course or two on 'ethics and CSR' is of no use unless they are included in all courses.

It is very encouraging to note the very recent work undertaken by Dr. Nancy Day of HW Bloch School of Business, University of Missouri and Dr. Joy Peluchette of University of Southern Indiana, through an extensive research to examine the extent to which HRM practices are perceived in business schools which they published in their paper aptly titled "How Business Schools Manage: Do They Practice What They Preach?". Effective HRM practices are especially important for service organizations where the satisfaction of the employee can influence the quality of service provided and the organization's ability to retain employees (Murphy 2003; Ulrich 1997; Voss, Tsikriktsis, Funk Yarrow and Owen 2005). Further, Nancy and Joy highlighted the following aspects in their paper:

- Business Schools are 'service' oriented
- Needs of all the stakeholders are to be addressed
- Administrators of business schools are poorly trained on the use of effective management tools.
- Accrediting bodies do not lay emphasis on sensitive HRM issues of faculty
- Notable exception reportedly is the University of Northern Colarados Monfort College of Business that won Malcolm Balridge award in 2004 for excellent performance in education (in addition to AACSB accreditation) which is an indication of sound HRM practices in place.
- Raising a pertinent question that while corporates reap benefits through effective HRM practices, are the business schools doing the same?
- Universities provide job security to faculty through 'tenure' system which limits their flexibility to lay the faculty off, should the situation so demand.
- Business schools are going in for hiring more 'professionally qualified' faculty rather than 'academically qualified' for faculty positions.
- Team based, flatter and decentralized, empowered decision making process have been found to be better than departments housed around functional disciplines.
- Pay increases have been significantly lower than what they were in non-academic sectors
- Surprisingly new hires were found to be paid 18 per cent higher than the presently serving (reward for leaving rather for loyalty?)
- No training in administrative duties for heads

- Reward systems were found to be more closely linked to outcomes in private schools than did those in state schools, while the latter scored high in selective hiring and empowerment.
- Finally the study highlighted that by and large majority of HRM practices were put to use by business schools with little attention to training and development and reward management systems.

Back home a recent study conducted by MeritTrac (2007) on 790 B-School graduates in six metro cities on key parameters concluded that 77 per cent of them are "unemployable". Lack of trained faculty, poor infrastructure, absence of on the field training, mediocre students are some of the reasons cited.

All the above studies and research point to one single factor, "you reap as you sow", i.e. good teachers turn out good students who in turn do good to the society and the cycle continues. But the 'quality' like charity has to begin at home. The review of literature also unfolds that very few studies have been undertaken on employees more so on faculty dimension of management institutes. Further majority of the literature or committees focused on general quality of management education without touching upon the need to exclusively articulate on recruitment and selection of good faculty, developing them through training and research, motivating them to give their best and then to retain them so that they become a kind of role models for their students, batch after batch. In fact there is hardly any management institute in our country which has a well laid out HR policy, manual or a properly organized HR department in place to take care of the HR related needs of the faculty and staff. HR function in most of the business schools of the country is more by 'default' than by 'design'.

PART II

4

Recruitment and Selection

The best recruitment strategy is word of mouth from your current employees. We have been getting lots of referrals from our employees.

– Jay Belew

The acquisition activity starts with Human Resource Planning (HRP) which 'is the process of anticipating, and making provision for the movement of people into, within, and out of an organization' (Bohlander & Snell 2005). Its purpose is to deploy the manpower resources as effectively as possible where and when they are needed in order to accomplish the organization's goals. In short, HRP is a kind of launchpad for all the other activities associated with HRM.

Once the required number and kind of human resources are determined, the management has to identify the places where the required manpower is available and then develop systems and procedures to attract them towards the organization before selecting suitable candidates for the job. This process is generally known as 'recruitment'. During this process efforts are made to inform the applicants fully about the qualifications required to perform the job and the career opportunities the organization can offer its employees. Whether a particular job vacancy will be filled by someone from within the organization or from outside will depend upon the availability of personnel, the organization's HR policies, and the requirements of the job to be staffed. Recruitment includes only finding the sources of prospective employees and stimulating them to apply for jobs. To that extent it is a kind of positive activity since it involves attracting as many applicants (both from within and outside) as possible. It is rather "a process to discover the sources of manpower to meet the requirements of the staffing schedule and to employ effective measures for attracting that manpower in any adequate number to facilitate effective selection of effective workforce".

After identifying sources of human resources for prospective employees and stimulating them to apply for jobs in an organization, the management has to perform next logical and sequential function of selecting the right employee for the right job, at the right place and time. In conjunction with the recruiting process which is designed to increase the number of applicants, whose qualifications meet job requirements and the needs of the organization, 'selection' is the process of reducing that number and choosing from among those individuals who have the relevant qualifications—the objective of selection is to choose the individual who can most successfully perform the job from the pool of qualified candidates. The selection procedure is the system of functions and devices adopted in a given company to ascertain whether the candidates' specifications match with the job specifications and requirements or not.

Selection of human resources is a critical and complex process. The ability of an organization to attain its goals effectively depends upon the effectiveness of its selection program. Selecting a right person and rejecting a wrong person is a kind of 'hit'. Whereas 'misses' are those which involve rejecting a right person also known as rejection error. Selecting a wrong person is known as selection error, and both the errors cost the organization dearly. Hence caution and care are to be exercised in this activity. 'Acquisition' as a HRM practice is of vital importance in any organization irrespective of its nature as long as the same is people intensive.

PLANNING

Failing to plan is planning to fail.

– Anon

Faculty is the largest component of manpower in a business school, and as such the discussion is basically confined to them only while excluding the administrative and support staff (non-teaching). Business schools all over the country and elsewhere are facing a severe shortage of faculty—shortage of qualified, for instance Ph.D. faculty, or in simple terms shortage of 'quality faculty'.

To start with, it is observed in business schools that certain amount of 'planning' takes place depending upon the student intake, expansion plans in terms of offering new programs, courses or electives and of course based on turnover of faculty due to lateral moves, sabbaticals for research or foreign assignments, etc. Planning also needs to be based on separation of faculty on retirement or move back to industry, etc. that is to say 'planning' per se has to be necessarily carried out. Since most of the business schools do not either have an exclusive HR department or a HR Manager/Executive, this function is carried out either at Head of the School or Head of the Academics levels or both of them get involved. Though 'planning' is an essential organizational function, generally management institutes fall short in this. In government sponsored institutes like IIMs and others or for those coming under university fold this activity even if undertaken, is not logically concluded due to reasons beyond institutional head's control. Paucity of funds or resource crunch or ban on further recruitment are the reasons normally cited. In case of privately run schools, generally unsaid but normally implied commercial orientation of their managements could be the reason for the heads of the institutions to shy away from this vital activity. The answer in both the cases lies in granting functional freedom to the head in staffing his outfit for a given teacher–student ratio which ideally is 1 : 10 for management education or a minimum of seven faculty members per school as per AICTE norms.

Manpower Planning

Manpower planning as a basic process of HRM has become very important in recent times for every organization and management institutes are no exception to this. It is the process of developing and determining objectives, policies and programs that will develop, utilize and distribute manpower so as to achieve the goals of the organizations. Dales Beach defines it as 'Human Resource Planning is a process of determining and assuring that the organizations will have an adequate number of qualified persons available at proper times, performing jobs which meet the needs of the enterprise and which provide satisfaction for the individuals involved.' A very comprehensive definition comes from Geisler (Edwin B Geisler), who said, 'Manpower planning is the process (including forecasting, developing, implementing and controlling) by which a firm ensures that it has the right number of people and right kind of people, at the right places at the right time, doing things for which they are economically most useful.' That is to say, to be effective, manpower planning must focus not only on the people involved but on the working conditions and relationships in which they work.

Manpower planning is a continuous process and it cannot be static or rigid. It needs to be flexible and amenable to modifications, review and adjustments in accordance with the needs of the organization or the changing circumstances. The process starts with understanding organizational objectives and translating them into a schedule of employee requirements over a period of time.

Our research indicated that close to 70 per cent of the business schools do undertake planning at one stage or the other.

Michael Armstrong (2006) subtly highlights the differences between human resource planning and manpower planning as the former is generally concerned with people skills, their development and deployment while the latter adopts a quantitative approach to deal only with their numbers. So 'HR planning' is a more appropriate term to denote planning activities for recruitment and retention of faculty, which ideally consists of demand and supply forecasting and their marrying up plans. The aim of this activity is much broader in the sense that more or less it includes almost the entire gamut of HRM, i.e. attract and retain people with relevant skill sets, anticipate surpluses or deficits, develop workforce to meet the changing needs, optimize the people utilization and institute an efficient retention strategy.

Based on the planning, a resourcing strategy is to be formulated, which should normally address the following (Michael Armstrong 2006)

- Requirement of faculty in each domain area/department
- Skill sets required
- Skill sets among the existing faculty
- Plans to meet the gaps in the above, if any
- Plans to develop or extend skill set base
- Plans to attract, develop, optimally utilize and retain faculty.
- Downsizing requirements if any.

DEPARTMENTAL COMMITTEE (HR/MARKETING/FINANCE AND INFORMATION TECHNOLOGY)

The first and the foremost activity is to establish a 'Departmental Committee' at each departmental level. ('Search Committee' in The University of California). The suggested constitution could be as under.

- Chairman – Head of the School/Establishment
- Presiding Officer – HOD/Dean/Professor (Ph.D.)
- Members
  1. Senior Faculty (Ph.D.)
  2. Senior Faculty (Ph.D.) from any other department
  3. Faculty (may or may not be Ph.D.)
  4. Faculty (may or may not be Ph.D.)
- Members Secretary – HR Manager of the School

The scope of the these departmental committees could be broadened to include various other issues apart from recruitment and selection such as:

- Research
- Welfare (Grievances, etc.)
- Discipline
- Seminars/conferences
- Library and intellectual resource base addition
- MDP/EDP/Consultancy Assignments
- Academic audit
- Curriculum review
- Accreditation norms
- Incentives, rewards and promotions
- Any other issue as assigned by the management

Points meriting attention by the Committee while addressing the above mentioned issues are:

- Presiding Officer shall conduct the proceedings and the Chairman may or may not attend them while retaining the power to ratify, approve or even reject the recommendations made therein, by the committee.
- HR Manager to form part of the committee only while dealing with the HR issues and could be excluded for others. One of the faculty members in that case may function as Member Secretary of the Committee.
- The committee's recommendations shall be in conformity with the existing laws of the land, as amended from time to time. HR Manager to provide the committee with complete information pertaining to 'statutory provisions' concerning all HR related issues.
- The committee to decide the periodicity of their meetings concerning various issues, and notify well in advance to all concerned so that staff can benefit from their sittings.

- The members of the committee could be rotated periodically so as to ensure objectivity and that every member of the faculty gets an opportunity to work in the committee.
- While dealing with issues related directly or indirectly to any member of the committee that particular member could be excluded during the conduct of the proceedings.
- Member from another department is expected to add value to the committee in terms of cross-functional competencies required for certain core and elective courses, and provide inputs on procedures followed in his parent department.

RECRUITMENT METHODS

With a machinery as suggested above in place to assist the Institutional Head in dealing with various academic or non-academic (HR/Admin) issues concerning faculty, the following recruitment methods could be considered. But before that it would be pertinent, to answer a question 'who is to be recruited?' Based on the research conducted on 'HRM practices' of business schools of our country, most widely accepted hierarchy of faculty in a particular department of a business school is

Table 4.1 Hierarchy of a Department of a Business School

↑
Dean/HOD
Deputy Dean/Professor
Associate Dean/Reader/Associate Professor
Senior Faculty Member/Assistant Professor
Faculty Member/Senior Lecturer
Faculty Associate/Lecturer
Research Associate/Teaching Assistant/Junior Lecturer

At the institutional level a Director may head the same (Dean, in case of certain schools following purely American system) and he may have a Principal too to assist him in academic affairs.

The hierarchy discussed above could be modified to suit the requirements of a particular school, specializations and electives offered.

Recruitment can take place for any of the levels mentioned above depending upon the requirement. Our research indicated that close to 80 per cent of the institutes resorted to 'advertisement' method, while 16 per cent went in for 'Employee reference and word of mouth approach, and barely 4 per cent opted for Recruitment Consultant mode to meet their recruitment needs. Having said that, various methods of recruitment that could be considered for implementation are discussed below:

Advertisements

Advertisements in the print media are the most popular and obvious method of attracting prospective faculty. But in these days of intense competition any 'run of the mill' advertisement is not likely to get the desired response. It has to be at its innovative best to attract attention, create and sustain interest and stimulate action to apply. A professional agency with expertise in handling advertisements of business schools must be chosen, and various models discussed before releasing the final version, which should be more in line with the perception of the candidate than that of the recruiter, while conforming to various statutory provisions. Time, place and the publication are equally important factors that have a bearing on the success of the advertisement.

E-Recruitment

Most revolutionary method of recruitment though more suitable for large organizations but could be used effectively for business schools too. Most ideal method is to have a link on the school web site titled as 'faculty recruitment' specifying all the details of a conventional print media advertisement and seek online response too from the prospective candidates. By far this is the least expensive method and the responses could be considered as an ongoing and continuous process of recruitment and vacancies filled up on need basis. Alternatively, job placement websites like Monster.com could be hired to put a 'post a job express' option in their website in which a job gets posted for a specified duration at a nominal cost, which would be a fraction of what it takes in a print media or hiring through a consultant. Both the above e-recruitment options especially the former, provide immediate access to a large number of prospective applicants. Suitable application templates could also be posted for filling up and submitting online.

E-recruitment has become so popular worldwide that 95 per cent of the companies in the US resort to it and GTE Corporation (Verizon) receive close to 30000 email resumes per year (John M. Ivancevich 2004).

Recruitment Consultant

This is the most expensive approach as most of the consultants charge a fee based on a percentage of the salary offered for the job sometimes even on annual basis. They render services like advertisement, sifting through the applications, preliminary interview and shortlisting. This reduces the workload of the business school to a considerable extent but the associated risks like huge costs and low quality applicants need to be kept in mind. Moreover the consultant looks at the process from his business angle and not from the client's organizational image point of view.

The school based recruiting process helps in boosting the image of the organization due to close involvement of the staff concerned, which may be compromised by a recruiting consultant.

Employee Reference

Some schools in India (16 per cent as per our research) follow this method which is fairly safe, good and could even be considered as the least expensive. A serving faculty member refers an acquaintance or a friend either engaged in the same profession (lateral hire) or someone with a flair for teaching interested in applying for a faculty position. Generally no bad cases get referred as the reputation of the referee would be at stake, in case of poor performance of the referred. This method has become quite popular as the author had seen teams of faculty members moving from one school to another en masse. Some schools have even instituted incentives to referees to be paid during the course of performance of the referred. The organizational culture plays a major role in this method. If the working environment is conducive to individual growth and development, contributing to raised levels of morale and motivation, every faculty member would like to undertake this exercise of referring suitable and promising candidates for various faculty positions in the school. This is a true win-win method.

Informal Methods

The process of attracting suitable and eligible candidates can also be undertaken through certain indirect methods. They are likely to motivate others to seek employment opportunities.

- Identifying suitable candidates during seminars/ conferences especially when they present papers and maintaining contact with them.
- Conducting inhouse seminars and other academic events and inviting industry experts and other academicians as delegates.
- Circulation of 'Newsletter' among industry and other business schools to give a feel of the student quality, and the prevailing work culture.
- Participation in 'job fairs' with display of publications of the faculty, etc.
- Increased 'industry interface' through guest lectures, projects, consultancy, sponsored seminars which may develop academic interests among corporate executives.
- Undertaking image boosting PR exercises like participating in TV talk shows, FM Radio interviews and interviews in education supplements of major newspapers.

- Frequent participation of faculty in the seminars discretely conveying the USPs and the prevailing conducive work environment of the school through well-designed presentations.

Visiting and Adjunct Faculty

Any discussion on recruitment and selection of business school faculty without touching upon the visiting and the adjunct faculty would be incomplete. They are also referred as part time or guest faculty. They form a vital part of the faculty base so much so that some of the private sector business schools function solely on the strength of these faculty members only, with a handful of permanent faculty for the keep sake. Certain advantages of having part time faculty are:

- They come from diverse backgrounds with varied experience which will add value to their teaching.
- Make up for the shortfalls in the faculty base
- Well suited for handling 'specialization' or elective courses
- Cost effective for the organization and minimal HR issues
- If from industry, they help in industry-interface, also they are generally more effective in teaching application techniques and case method of teaching, etc.
- They are adept at counseling students on career options and its management.
- If from an academics background, they generally are 'experts' in their chosen field and the students derive benefit from their knowledge and skills.
- Advantages of this faculty accrue more to the schools located amidst corporate offices in the city.

However, just as every coin has two sides, part time faculty system has its own downside.

- No organizational loyalties or sense of belongingness
- Relationship with the school is purely transactional
- Bonding with the students will be limited or even nil at times

- Student evaluation may or may not be fair
- Tendency to neglect academic rigour and schedules due to various other commitments.
- Lack of or minimal contribution to institutional image building process
- Intellectual property or resource base of the school may take a dent.
- Lack of continuity in teaching due to frequent lateral moves mostly on financial considerations.

In view of above, due caution and care are to be exercised before employing part time faculty. Employing a handful of them possessing extraordinary skills is however unavoidable and even advisable for any school, not withstanding the numbers of their permanent faculty. Recruitment in their case would be mostly 'reference and word of mouth' method while all the methods discussed for selecting a regular faculty could also be applied for selecting a guest faculty too. The compensation could be on 'per session basis' or on a monthly basis for those who spend full two or three days in a week in the school, in which case they are normally referred as 'adjunct faculty'. Any method can be adopted depending upon the requirement and mutual understanding and convenience.

"One needs to understand the distinction between availability of human resources to serve as faculty and recruitment of good faculty. The observation that is often made is that good faculty is scarce. But, at the same time, the question arises why should we expect to get readymade good faculty only? Why cannot we have a slight shift in our stand by owning up the responsibility to develop the available willing resources who are not only willing to serve as faculty but have a distinct potential for development into good faculty. Careful screening and selection of the right person, therefore becomes crucially important. Merit should not be compromised at any cost. Qualifications should not be relaxed. Good faculty is not necessarily available with the industry (U Dhar 2004)."

SELECTION

If you pick the right people and give them the opportunity to spread their wings and put compensation as a carrier behind it, you almost don't have to manage them.

– Jack Welch

Selection is the process by which an organization chooses from a list of applicants the person or persons who best meet the selection criteria for the position available (John M. Ivancevich). Business Schools have a mandate to deliver quality education so that managerial effectiveness becomes a way of life in the industry. To that extent these schools are under an obligation to provide quality managerial resource to the corporates. Here it is pertinent to make a mention of all the stakeholders involved in the process. They are:

- Management of the school
- Students and parents
- Faculty and admin staff
- Industry
- Regulatory bodies
- Society in general

Expectations of each group from the other are interlinked and are aplenty. By and large faculty forms the most important part of the stakeholders' community since he would be the one moulding the student into a productive executive. A management teacher has a different role to play in doing so in the sense, apart from teaching the subject knowledge he should also impart the application technique and finally must ensure that the student becomes a well rounded personality at the end of his stay in the institute. It's a kind of three dimensional approaches KAP (Knowledge, Application and Personality) as far as his deliverables to a student are concerned. Similarly one needs to be conscious of the feedback received from the affected parties. A delivery and feedback model for a typical business school is shown below.

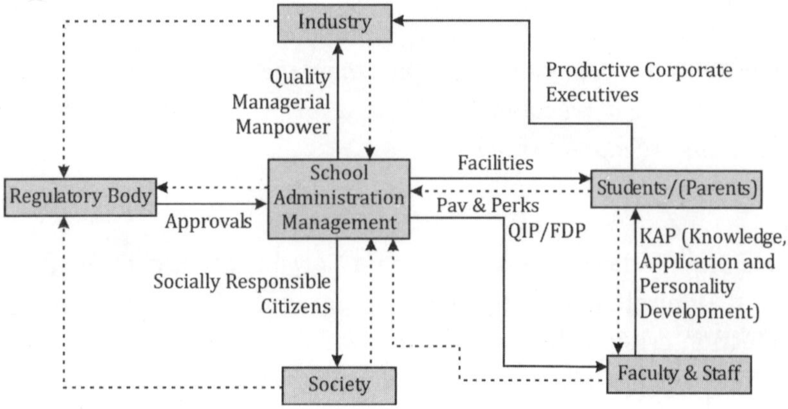

Fig. 4.1 Delivery (⟶) & Feedback (····➤) Model of a typical Business School

Now the question arises as to what does an individual faculty need to deliver as expected above.

He needs a set of competencies, (through QIP – Quality Improvement Programs or FDPs) both at base level and those that can further be built upon. A faculty is basically expected to undertake the following activities to sharpen his skill set for KAP.

- Continuous updating of his subject knowledge
- Research and publication
- Executive training, consultancy and projects
- Industry interface and institution building
- Soft skills

  (*The major business schools produce graduates with analytical horsepower and solid command of the basics – finance, marketing and strategy. But soft skills such as communication, leadership, and team mentality sometimes receive cursory treatment – Wall Street Journal*)
- Imparting of entrepreneurial skills.

The education of the global citizen, one who will be comfortable, visiting, working and living in diverse countries is the responsibility of the academia.

– Lundstrum & Schuster (1988)

A suggested competency based HR model for faculty selection and retention is given below.

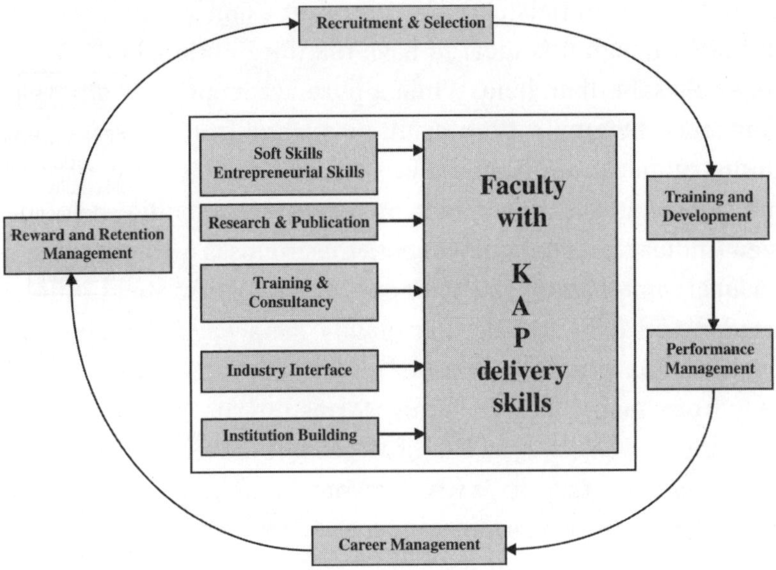

(KAP – Knowledge, Application and Personality development)

Fig. 4.2 A competency based HR model for a typical business school

Before embarking upon the actual selection process it is necessary to define the requirements in terms of job descriptions and specifications and deciding on the terms and conditions of employment. It would be ideal for the selection committee to have the above data prepared well in advance for each position of the departmental hierarchy, before the actual selection starts. This will help to understand what contributes to high job performance. Also, there is a need to categorize applicants into various groups as under so as to match them with the actual requirements.

- Fresh applicants
- Applicants with academic experience, with and without doctoral qualifications
- Applicants with corporate exposure only
- Applicants with both corporate and academic exposure.

There is a neverending debate on what constitutes the qualitative requirement of a management teacher, i.e. pure academic credentials or only corporate experience, or a blend of both. Though it is ideal to have the third option, but it would be easily said than done. While a pure academician is strong on concepts, the application techniques come from a person with industry background only and both are equally important for management education. Thus a 60 per cent (academic) and 40 per cent (industry) distribution of both the groups is recommended as an ideal combination for a business school. (Dharni Sinha 2004). It needs no further emphasis that 'quality' has always been a problem in this country and more so of quality education which comes only from quality faculty. Faculty forms the core of management education. James Libig author of Merchants of Vision identified six management perspectives which involve enhancing social equality, protecting natural environment, enabling human activity, serving higher purposes, ethical behaviour and personal transformation (CL Singh – WTO & Competitiveness, Challenges for Indian Business and Management Education – Excel Books 2001 P. 160). These perspectives were developed after studying scores of business executives spread across 14 countries.

On the quantitative front it is essential to have a teacher student ratio of 1 : 10 so as to ensure optimum mutual attention. Any compromise on the required number of faculty which generally is the case in our business schools (due to shortage of qualified and quality faculty) is likely to result in a poor quality turn out of students.

The aim of the above discussion is to highlight the critical need to select an eligible and a suitable faculty member.

SELECTION METHODS

Sow an action
You reap a habit
Sow a habit
You reap a character
Sow a character
You reap a destiny

– William James (Harvard Teacher)

Following selection methods could be considered for implementation:

- ***Application Blanks and Preliminary Screening:***
  A school can design its own application blank depending upon the type of information that it needs to solicit from the candidates. Generally they deal with the biographical information of the candidate like education, work experience and specialized training received, etc. The Recruitment and Selection (R&S) or the departmental committee sifts the received application forms by comparing them with the key criteria in the job specification, position wise and sorts them into three groups: good, average and poor. The 'average' category could be gone through again to assess if they can be graduated to 'good' list. Thus a short list of good potential candidates is made.
  In view of the criticality of selecting a quality faculty who is both eligible from qualifications and experience point of view and suitable from performance on the job, view point, the committee could ask the candidate to submit a handwritten note along with the application blank which could be called the 'Hiring Template for a Business School Faculty'. It basically deals with the ideas and perceptions of a candidate about the profession he is planning to pursue. The candidate could be asked to respond in point form

(a minimum of five and a maximum of ten) for each question. The aim of this document is three fold.

- Social structure of a human being can be studied through his handwriting, and graphology as a selection aid is being used extensively all over the world. (Fowler 1991 a)
- As per Psychologists the handwritten answers to various questions generally indicate the candidates' general tendency towards the job, with not many deviations.
- Acts as a shortlisting tool for the R&S committee.

(**Note:** The doubtful responses if noticed could be cross-checked during the actual interview)

The template is suggested to be on the following lines.

Table 4.2 A model of 'Hiring Template for a Business School Faculty'

1. What is your concept of a Management Teacher and Passionate teaching?
2. Name the books and the authors you normally refer in your functional area.
3. How do you plan to deal with difficult or weak students?
4. What soft skills you think you possess?
5. Indicate your research and publication activity in the last two years.
6. How do you propose to impart knowledge and its application to students?
7. What is your idea of 'character building' of a person?
8. How do you plan to maintain industry interface?
9. How can you contribute to 'institutional image building' process?
10. What are your views on 'Management Education in India'?

Demo Lecture

This is a high validity test for assessing person job fit, where a candidate is made to take an actual class either for a live set of students or for the R&S committee. Shortlisted candidates could be put through this test. 80 per cent of the business schools studied by us follow this method. Certain aspects to be kept in mind for adopting this method:

- Candidate to be given the topic by the department and adequate time to prepare for it.
- To be given adequate time for actual presentation making the necessary facilities available.
- Preferably to be conducted in the presence of R&S Committee, in a live classroom like a normal class and a random feedback from the students could also be considered.
- A grilling question and answer session at the end is essential.

Interviews

Based on the outcome of Demo Lecture a candidate is interviewed by the R&S Committee. Of the business schools researched by us 85 per cent adopt this method. Again this is a high validity test for a person job fit with moderate validity for assessing person group or organization fit. Structured interviews are suitable so that the committee members are well in sync with each other. This is an ideal platform to cross check the responses of the candidate for various questions of the 'HR Template' suggested above.

Further preplanned standard questions to test the depth of the subject knowledge and of contemporary thoughts could be asked which would highlight the specific skills and competencies relevant to the job. A situational or behavioural question like "what if a student is unruly in class...." could also be asked to probe into student management or handling capacity.

Psychometric Tests

Only 3 per cent of the institutes that we studied conduct these tests. The purpose of these tests is to provide an objective means of measuring individual abilities or characteristics. They enable the selectors to decide the extent to which a person shall be successful on the job. Smith and Roberstonson (1986) define a psychological test as 'a carefully chosen, systematic and standardized procedure for evolving a sample of responses from candidates which can be used to assess one or more of their psychological characteristics with those of a representative sample of an appropriate population'. The 'HR Template' suggested earlier more or less meets this requirement well before getting on to the actual selection process.

- On successful completion of the above stages a candidate may be seen by the institutional head in his capacity as the Chairman of the R&S committee where an unstructured interview could take place resulting in either approval or rejection of the R&S committee recommendations.

Reference Checks

Once a candidate has been found to be suitable for a job offer, reference checks are made from his previous employers, or coworkers with or without the knowledge of the candidate. Barely 12 per cent of the schools studied by us undertake this exercise. Most of the time only a positive image of the candidate comes up during these checks as the lists are generated by candidates themselves. Hence it is suggested to carry out a discrete check from past students and unlisted colleagues if possible at school level only as hiring of professional agencies for this would be a very expensive proposition.

POINTS TO PONDER

- A board member refers a fresh MBA graduate from a low key business school to the Director/Dean for induction as Faculty Member, in one of the departments. As Recruitment and Selection (R&S) Committee member how do you propose to deal with the situation, when both HOD and Director feel that the board member should be obliged?
- With a large new batch of students scheduled to join in a month's time, as HOD you are under great pressure to recruit new faculty as suddenly a lot of unexpected lateral movement of faculty has taken place in the last couple of

months. There was a kind of mass exodus to a new business school opened in the neighborhood. As HOD and Presiding officer of R&S Committee of your department, how do you propose to deal with this problem?

- An old student of the school approaches the Director for a job as he loses his due to recession and his father dies in a road accident. With a couple of siblings still in the college, the young man presents a pathetic picture of himself. You are the Director of the School and the recession has hit the school too. What do you plan to do and why?

SUMMING UP

By and large one of the serious problems that is being confronted in the management education field today is the shortage of talented and qualified faculty, and the critical need to take up proper planning and resorting to various methods of attracting and selecting most suitable ones as against the most eligible. Eligibility is the meeting of quantitative requirements of a job while suitability deals with the actual delivery on the job. The entire R&S activity is depicted in the chart below.

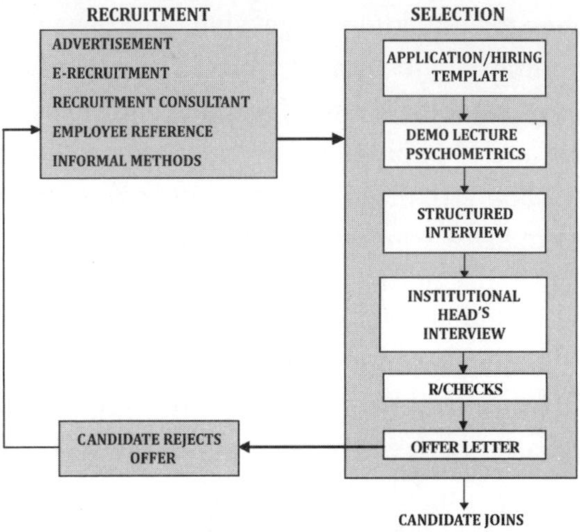

Fig. 4.3 R&S chart for a business school

5
Training and Development

Training is everything. The peach was once a bitter almond; cauliflower is nothing but cabbage with college education.

– Mark Twain

Every organization needs to have well trained and experienced people to perform its varied activities. If the existing employees can squarely meet their job requirement then training may not be all that important, but with the constantly changing business models, there will be corresponding changes in the requirements of skill sets of people or the employees. Hence it is necessary to raise the skill levels and increase the versatility and adoptability of employees.

Training in general sense refers to a planned effort by a company to facilitate employees learning of job related competencies. These competencies include knowledge, skill, and behaviours that are critical for successful job performance. The goal of training is for employees to master the knowledge, skills, and behaviours relevant to their jobs and to apply them to day-to-day activities. It is now being increasingly realized that to gain competitive advantage, training has to involve more than just basic skill development.

Training has become increasingly vital to the success of modern organizations, which normally compete on competencies, the core sets of knowledge and expertise that give them an edge over their competitors. Training plays a central role in nurturing and strengthening these competencies and in this way it has become a part of strategy implementation. There is a need to understand the terms training and development in correct perspective as they normally tend to be associated with any learning activity. Experts distinguish between 'training', which tends to be more narrowly focused and oriented towards short-term performance concerns (that is basically preparing an employee to perform his present job effectively) and 'development' which tends to be oriented more towards broadening an individual's skills for the future responsibilities. These two terms tend to be combined into a single phrase 'training and development' to recognize the combination of activities used by organizations to increase the skill base of employees.

TRAINING AND DEVELOPMENT IN BUSINESS SCHOOLS

Given the fact that the jobs are becoming increasingly complex the importance of employee training has increased many folds. When jobs were simple, easy to learn and influenced by only a small degree of technological changes and stable in content, there was little need for employee training. But the rapid changes taking place due to liberalization, privatization and globalization during the last decade and half in India, ever since the economic reforms were initiated in 1991, have mounted pressure on organizations to change themselves, in the way the products are made, serviced and offered. The emergence of services sector further fueled the need to alter things, and hence the jobs, and the skills that are required are also changing. Business schools are no different and cannot remain complacent to these changes in the business scenario since industry is the direct consumer of the products put out by business schools. Late Peter Drucker; in his essay "The Age of Social Transformation" argues that "We are in the midst of the most extreme societal changes in the recorded history. These changes now in turn pose a challenge to the way we manage our institutions, where there is a strong need to unlearn, learn and relearn as to how to adopt to the new environment on a continuous basis". Hence training function as such becomes important in business schools too.

In business schools much emphasis is laid on training and development because the academic has to keep pace with the changes taking place in technology, business, products and services. The rate of obsolescence of technology in IT & ITES sectors is very high. Manufacturing techniques have undergone a tremendous change and services sector with its innovative ideas has gone ahead. Consequently, business management graduates entering various sectors need to be fully prepared to meet the emerging challenges. Hence the upgradation of skills by management faculty assumes critical importance. Opportunities for learning are also a significant need of the faculty, and hence catering to this need is very important for the growth and development of management education in this country. As knowledge workers, faculty prefers to learn subjects of their own discipline first in preference to the general management subjects.

In business schools training is imparted through Faculty Development Programs (FDPs) to hone the skills for the present job. Non-doctoral faculties are encouraged to take up research work leading to the award of Ph.D. degree. Doctoral faculty are asked to take up post-doctoral research work either to widen their existing knowledge base or make a foray into the areas not their own (cross discipline knowledge). IBS for example regularly conducts FDPs during summer months and every faculty member is expected to attend at least one FDP in a year. Non-doctoral faculty are expected to enroll for Ph.D. and complete it in 3 to 4 years, failing which they will not be confirmed in their service or subjected to similar such measure. Developmental activities also take place in terms of encouraging and insisting upon the faculty to publish articles in magazines and journals and present papers in seminars either at regional, national or international level. This is done through quarterly research group meetings for each discipline wherein faculty's previously committed 'intellectual contribution' is measured against actually achieved figures and reasons for short falls are analysed. Faculty members are also given adequate incentives for publishing articles, writing cases, research papers, editing magazines/journals, presenting papers in seminars, etc. Yet another activity which is very specific to IBS on intellectual development side is publishing of 'derivative books' by faculty members as consulting editors. IBS faculty has developed more than 600 books in the last six years or so.

Premier business schools like IIMs, XLRI, SP Jain, and MDI, etc. regularly conduct EDP/MDPs with the help of their faculty, which in a way contributes to the intellectual development of their own faculty. Organized training programs exclusively for the internal faculty are also conducted in number of institutions coming both under university system or private managements. These training programs are generally sponsored either by AICTE or UGC. However faculty members are also permitted to attend the FDPs conducted by other institutions.

DEVELOPMENT AND SKILL UPGRADATION IN FACULTY

The fact that there is a huge shortage of faculty needs no further debate. Under the circumstances, wisdom lies in retaining the existing and training them to meet the changing requirements of the curricula. Most of the teachers need to orient their teaching skills to suit the management education in the first place. Yet another area is the lack of cross-functional business knowledge as faculty generally tend to limit themselves to their own area only. Also, academic faculty needs to familiarize themselves with the application techniques of the theoretical concepts by taking up case discussions, case writings, projects and consultancy assignments, etc. To that extent an academic faculty could even be considered to stay with the companies during the projects or internship of the students which will be serving two purposes. Firstly he would be able to supervise the projects of the students from close quarters as faculty guide, in association with the 'company guide' and secondly he would also gain the first hand experience of a company's overall functioning with all its departments duly integrated to achieve a common objective. Similarly industry may send their executives to business schools to deliver guest lectures on 'ground realities' of the theoretical concepts taught in the class. Jamnalal Bajaj Institute of Management takes maximum advantage of this concept by adjusting the time tables to suit the conveniences of the working executives. Also, faculty need to be interacted with by HOD/ Principal/Dean/Director in relation to the 'performance standards' set (Chapter 7) so as to indentify and meet the developmental needs on a continuous basis and not when it is too late to do anything.

Alliances with local or outside business schools are essential and augurs well for the faculty as they network and exchange knowledge by joint writing or presenting of papers. A month long QIP or FDP during academic lull periods (April–May) will prove beneficial. Also, faculty work norms in terms of teaching load need to be regularly reviewed keeping in view the other intellectual, self-development or institution image building activities one is engaged in. A research culture as discussed in Chapter 6 needs to be created in the school.

... high achievement in formal education is no guarantee of the ability to apply that knowledge while wide experience is not guarantee of knowledge, understanding or competence.

– Jennifer Tann 1995

INDIVIDUAL LEARNING

It takes a life time of learning to realize the extent of our ignorance. Learning is a life long process both at individual and at organizational level. Every organization more so an educational institution must facilitate the learning of its individual members and in the process ensure its own complete transformation. The over emphasis on qualifications and experience during recruitment and selection process often results in failure to raise a relevant question 'what did you learn last year and what are you planning to learn this year'. The opportunity to indicate to the candidate that the institution not only encourages life long learning but even demands it, thus gets lost, by default. Generally the older academic staff tend to be little arrogant about their professional knowledge and skills ("We are highly professional, we all are good teachers" is an often heard remark) and this sets a wrong precedence among the younger lot, which needs to be curbed. Peter Senge introduces (1990: II) the model of five disciplines for individual learning and development.

- Personal mastery
- Mental models
- Shared vision
- Group learning
- Systems thinking

The teacher is an intellectual who engages students in the process of producing knowledge.

– Paulo Freire

ORGANIZATIONAL LEARNING

Collective learning process results in change of the behaviour of an organization thus becoming a learning one and no collective learning would be possible without learning at individual levels. Though individual learning is a fundamental pre-requisite for organizational learning, but it is not a sufficient condition. Apart from learning, people need to co-operate, with each other and 'adopt a consultative approach' to plan and do things. For a typical business school the learning can be a 'single loop', one, when it say reduces the fee structure in response to declining number of students, while 'double loop' learning involves not only changes in rules but also in the basic assumptions, like review of curriculum if any or of the prevailing collegiate atmosphere, etc. Double loop learning is a more involved process with far reaching consequences. 'Triple loop' learning is something like a thorough 'overhaul' of the system wherein the role, mission, vision and the processes may undergo drastic changes. Generally business schools limit themselves to single or double loop learning only.

IDENTIFICATION OF TRAINING AND DEVELOPMENT NEEDS

To make sure that training is timely and focused on priority issues authorities of business schools must approach needs assessment systematically by utilizing different types of analysis at organizational, task and personal levels. US organizations reportedly spend $60 billion annually on training most of which gets wasted due to unsystematic methods used. A study by American Society for Training and Development (ASTD) indicates that training needs assessment is undertaken in less than 50 per cent cases, before initiating a training program. But ironically as the speed of change increases and time and resources are at a premium, the need for good needs assessment actually increases. As we said the first step is to assess the needs at the business school (organizational) levels to determine where exactly the training emphasis should be placed. Next the organization must carefully analyse the actual duties of the faculty in order to determine their training needs and this is what is called task level analysis. Finally we need to assess the training needs at the individual level where a particular faculty may need training in soft skills, teaching methodologies, case discussion, evaluation methods, etc. Yet another area of concern in the area of training, for management faculty is their 'competency assessment', as knowledge workers. This is to examine whether they are updating their skills and knowledge in proportion to the changing requirements of the business so that the students do not enter the companies with a totally outdated and obsolete knowledge base. This is of special significance to the management faculty as their job is knowledge intensive. While carrying out 'person analysis' it is equally essential to identify those who do not need the training as more often than not they will also be sent for training as a routine practice along with the others who need it. This would result in a huge wastage of resources.

Business Schools also use performance appraisal information, as inputs for training need analysis. However while performance appraisals may reveal who is not meeting expectations, it typically does not reveal why. If performance deficiencies are due to ability problems training may likely be a good intervention. However if performance deficiencies are due to poor motivation or factors outside an employee's control, training may not be the answer. In that case personal discussion across the table is the only solution.

Our research has indicated that training and development needs are being identified in 70 per cent of the business schools.

MEETING THE TRAINING NEEDS

Identification of training needs is just one half of the story, the other being the actual meeting of the needs which is as important. Otherwise the relevance of identification of needs is lost. Once the training needs have been identified and determined, the next logical step is to go about in designing the type of learning environment necessary to enhance learning process. The success of any training program largely depends more on the ability of the organization to identify the correct training needs. Success hinges on taking the information, gained from need analysis and utilizing it to design first rate training programs. Experts (Bohlander & Snell 2005) believe that training design should focus on at least four related issues, i.e. objectives, readiness and motivational levels of the trainees, basics of learning and skills of the trainers. If one is not sure as to what one wants to achieve as the outcome of a training program then it would be an exercise in futility. Same goes for the receptivity and the enthusiasm/motivational levels of the trainees without which one would end up talking to benches and chairs.

Training has to build a bridge between employees and the organization. One important step in this direction is giving full consideration to the psychological principles of learning that is the characteristics of training programs that help employees grasp new material, make sense of it in their own lives, and transfer it back to the job. The areas where management faculty needs training are:

- Teaching skills upgradation by leveraging on technology
- Updating of knowledge in own area
- Research and publication
- Case method of teaching
- Evaluation instruments
- Soft skills
- Integrated approach to business and application of concepts
- Orientation to management education
- Institution building activities

"The faculty should not be restricted to teaching only. The multiple roles of a teacher in a professional institution cannot be undermined. A teacher cannot afford to end up as a classroom operator ... Involvement in institution building activities should be facilitated."

– (U Dhar 2004)

More often than not some good business schools conduct FDPs generally covering all the above areas and faculty from the middle/lower rung institutes attend these FDPs. The issue here is, the faculty so nominated to attend the FDP may or may not need training either in some or in any of the areas being covered and that's where the gap between identification and meeting of the training needs comes into play. Conducting and attending FDPs is undertaken more as a routine activity than as a developmental measure 'Continuous Faculty Development should be seen as an investment not as an expenditure' (U Dhar 2004).

Our research has indicated that though T&D needs are being identified in 70 per cent of the cases, but they are actually being met in 25 per cent of the cases only thus there is a large gap between identification and meeting of training needs which should be bridged. Paucity of funds and inability on the part of the managements to spare faculty from teaching load are quoted as possible reasons for this state of affairs which must be addressed for effective academic functioning.

The areas of training mentioned above could be grouped under the following types:

- Induction training
- Orientation training
- Refresher courses
- Workshops
- Industry training
- Faculty Development Programs (FDPs)

Induction Training

Training given at the start of one's career to acclimatize oneself to the new environment. Fresh inductees like Research Associates, Teaching Assistants and Faculty Associates or Junior Lecturers could be put through this module. Brief contents could be

- Discussion on school's vision and mission
- Role of the inductee
- Organization structure and working culture
- Teaching and research climate
- Career progression
- Systems and processes
- Admin and HR issues

(Suggested duration: 5 working days and to include a test at the end)

Orientation Training

Generally organized for experienced faculty who move laterally and enter the organization for the first time. The objective is to acquaint them with the organizational culture with special emphasis on teaching and research as they form the life line of academic fraternity in business school. General contents of this training program could be

- Contents of induction training program discussed above duly modified to suit the experienced faculty
- Teaching methodology and expectations
- Research and publications and expectations
- Student evaluation systems
- Student feedback linkages
- Institution building activities and expectations
- Industry interface
- Miscellaneous academic and non-academic roles

(Suggested duration: One to two weeks with at least two tests)

Workshops

These training programs are focused on a single theme to establish a proper link between theory and practice. Following are the areas in which workshops for duration of 2 to 3 days could be conducted for faculty:

- Soft skills
- Mentoring and counseling skills
- Classroom and student management
- Case study method of teaching
- Student evaluation instruments
- Listening skills
- Environment and sustainable development
- Business ethics and value systems
- Innovative teaching methods and role plays
- Research methodology and databases
- Statistical analysis and hypothesis testing
- Undertaking consultancy assignments

Refresher Courses

These are normally conducted departmentally for the faculty of that department to familiarize the faculty with the latest developments that are taking place in their functional discipline. There is no need to have a separate Resource Person or an Instructor but faculty members themselves must prepare presentations and deliver them to their colleagues in the department, which could be later converted into either research papers or magazine articles. One day in a month could be catered for this professional development activity, which would be intellectually stimulating and challenging if organized properly. By far this is the least expensive training method.

Industry Training

Pure academic faculty with no industry exposure tends to restrict themselves , to teaching the application techniques as mentioned in the textbooks. To that extent, this becomes a little handicap in their teaching as management students generally seek more convincing examples based on ground realities. Academic faculty are also found to be lacking in business sense and integrated approach to business through various functional areas like finance, marketing, HR and IT. Knowledge of actual functioning of a business unit on the ground is highly essential for any business school faculty for effective dissemination of knowledge without which teaching would be reduced to a mere vocal delivery of bookish facts. Such faculty should be assigned to companies where the students pursue projects.

Faculty Development Programs (FDPs)

These form the crux of faculty training and development activity in a business school. They could be theme based or general management based. The objective is both professional and personal development as a cross section of topics are addressed by experts in the field. They also facilitate peer group learning as faculty from other business schools are invited to attend. The duration again could range from a minimum of one week to a maximum of three weeks. Topics generally covered are:

- Managerial effectiveness
- Academic co-ordination/administration
- Research and publication
- Case method of teaching
- Intellectual and transformational leadership of educational institutions
- Student management and their assessment methods
- Industry interface and their expectations
- Role of stakeholders and their expectations
- Economy of the country and role of management education
- Business school rankings
- Accreditation standards
- Conduct of national and international seminars/conferences
- Institutional image building processes
- Role of social sciences and liberal arts in management education
- Environmental sciences
- Personality development measures
- Significance of cross-functional knowledge in improving managerial effectiveness

The list could be endless, and the business school head in consultation with his academic advisors (HODs) may identify newer areas of topical interest which have a bearing on business, society and environment in general and on management education in particular.

MISCELLANEOUS AND INFORMAL TRAINING METHODS

All the training and development methods discussed above are formal in nature involving considerable money, time and effort and not so well established business schools may not be able to undertake them on their own. However, faculty development oriented business schools can resort to any of the following training method to ensure faculty's growth and professional development.

- Sponsoring faculty to attend FDPs conducted by well-established schools like IIMs, XLRI, MDI, IBS and IITs (Schools of Management)
- Sponsoring faculty to attend seminars/conferences at regional/national/international levels by presenting papers
- Providing suitable incentives for target based publication activities
- Reimbursing cost of undertaking M.Phil./Ph.D. programs as private candidates
- Sparing faculty to undertake fieldwork for research
- Provision of infrastructural facilities in terms of wide band Internet, and adequate library resources both on- and off-line
- Running of inhouse newsletters, magazines and journals
- Encouragement to publish reviews/summaries of books dealing with contemporary management thoughts
- Mentoring and coaching by senior faculty

To sum up, it would be pertinent to remember what Jean Paul Satre the famous philosopher had said 'Man is not the sum of what he has already but rather the sum of what he does not yet have, of what he could have'.

6
Research and Consultancy

"Research is to teaching as sin is to confession, unless you participate in the former; you have little to say in the latter."

– John Slaughter

None could have been more right in highlighting the importance of research as an intellectual activity or better even as a survival factor for the academic fraternity. Late Dharni P Sinha an accomplished management educator expressed a similar sentiment by saying "the hall mark of higher education is not only dissemination of learning but generation of knowledge which will remain an important challenge in the coming decades". In the overzealous and frantic expansion of management education, the promoters and administrators have regrettably lost sight of the basic tenet of higher education, i.e. research to generate knowledge. In the last fifty odd years of existence of management education in our country, there is really nothing much to claim or to write home about in this field. The number of Ph.D. scholars we churned out in management discipline is pathetically low when compared to the ever rising number of business schools we are talking about. The efforts to research and publish have been more on individual basis rather as an institutionally supported activity. That is to say that the business schools have done precious little to advance management knowledge as such, either through basic research or applied research. Most of the institutions do not have a culture that support or encourage research.

To start with a 'research culture' has to be ingrained into the core culture of the institutions with a research community and an agenda. A support system in terms of adequate library resources both on- and off-line, sufficient funds, reduced teaching loads and incentives, etc. needs to be created in every business school. Indian management faculty members do undertake little research and whatever there is, it neither reaches the practicing manager nor enters the teaching curriculum (SL Rao 2009). There is a strong need to fuel imagination and ignite creative thinking among management students which is more important than knowledge per se, and faculty have little or no choice but to be research oriented themselves and indulging in it in the first place. If 'the business Ph.D. is an endangered species' (Jennifer Merrit 2004) in the US it is a rare commodity in India. Despite producing anything between 1000 and 1500 business Ph.Ds. every year, the US is going to face shortage of 2500 doctoral faculties by 2012 as projected by the Doctoral Faculty Commission to the AACSB and our short falls would be many times over, given the low rate at which they are turned out here.

The question then arises about the 'relevance' of the research undertaken. The AACSB categorizes it into three segments; 'discipline based' which is purely theoretical and it may or may not find its way into practice, 'applied' research that serves the practitioners and the 'pedagogical' that is basically used to add value to teaching. It needs no debate to say that business schools are generally evaluated based on the quality of research carried out by their faculty members. This is where the 'applied' research takes the cake when it is conducted scientifically and with relevance and accessibility to practitioners who should benefit from it. Unfortunately most of the academics go in for 'discipline' based theoretical research, even when the accreditation agencies insist that business schools must demonstrate the value of their faculties' research not by volumes (page counts and citations), but by the impact it makes in the workplace. That is to say the research should expand the boundaries of applicable knowledge by first raising unasked questions and then answering them. 'The research is almost universally unread by real world managers' is an understatement to say the least as most of it is quantitative, hypothesis driven and esoteric. A paper in a 2006 issue of "Strategy & Leadership" remarked that 'research is not designed with managers' needs in mind, nor is it communicated in the journals they read thus most of it becoming self referential closed system, irrelevant to corporate performance. Yet another dimension of the research is its relevance to the society at large, like carrying an aspirin in wallet for emergency use in a cardiac event or even glucose during hypoglycemia for that matter. Though these facts were known for long, doctors have now only started realizing the value of scientifically supported findings and the evidence provided by research to recommend such things to the patients.

Patrick Barwise of London Business School comes out with a concept called 'inductive research'—a study which proceeds without preconceived notions, observing organizational behaviour in its true form and then draw conclusions on what it finds—is more likely to be practiced in the real world than any other kind. But the downside to this is the sneers it draws from the editors of academic journals on which most of the faculty depend for publication of their research work. This calls for a major reform and a change of mindset among management gurus at the editorial desks of such journals. Fortunately saving grace comes in the form of MBA rankings by Financial Times and Business Week who now score schools on their contribution to both journals they consider purely 'academic' and ones they consider 'practitioner', i.e. ones managers might read (Economist.com 2007). Thus there is a dire need to close the gap between research and practice. Robert J Grossman a contributing editor of HR Magazine and a professor at Marist College in Poughkeepsie, New York in his treatise 'Close the Gap Between Research and Practice' (HR Magazine Nov 2009) highlights the need for the corporate to be more patient in understanding and valuing research, differentiate between an opinion and an evidence based conclusion and finally be flexible and open minded to new ideas researchers generate.

The learned professor makes useful and simple suggestions in this regard.

- Adhere to AACSB's standards on faculty's scholarship
- Review curriculum to include evidence based management
- Involve consultants or indulge in consultancy
- Faculty and practitioners to become partners in research through conferences or thinktank sessions
- Get the research sponsored by the Industry
- Social relationships with the corporates foster knowledge transfer

"It is in fact nothing short of a miracle that the modern methods of instruction have not yet entirely strangled the holy curiosity of inquiry."

– Albert Einstein

Yet another important feature of 'research' in business schools is the role it plays in their rankings. Studies have indicated that business school research is significantly correlated with rankings and it forms the very foundation of school's prestige. Research also appears to affect prospective students' perceptions in their selections of schools (JS Armstrong and Ted Sperry 1994). This is based on the belief that faculty research adds value to his teaching and thus makes him a better teacher. Then comes the issue of quality or success of research and the methods to measure it. There are various schools of thought, on parameters to measure quality and success, i.e. size of the publication (page count), number of publications (volume), journal of publications (refereed or otherwise), or the citations the article or the paper receives, etc. which are mostly academic in nature and generally do not consider the business or social relevance of the research product.

An ideal research product should lead to another research to that extent it is not an end product but only an intermediate one. Stan J Liebowitz of University of Texas in Dallas, USA, says that there is only one method of measuring research success, i.e. by the number of citations that a faculty member receives from other researchers, which indicates the impact of ones' research on others. While in the West so much of importance is attached to quality research by both accreditation and ranking agencies the situation in India is far different. Research forms part of the intellectual capital (Indian Management – AIMA rankings Oct 2009) or academic excellence parameter (Outlook Sep 28, 2009), and only Business Today puts 'high quality research paper' among top of the 'faculty' parameter (Oct 18, 2009). Not much emphasis is laid on the 'citations' (Qualitative) part of the research by most of the ranking or accreditation agencies while looking at its quantitative aspects. 'Impact of Research' a taskforce report of the AACSB authored by luminaries of INSEAD, University of Chicago, Ohio State, UCLA and University of Rochester, highlights the following salient points (Dean Bruner's Blog, Website of University of Virginia, Darden School of Business, etc.).

- 'Research' to denote forms of 'scholarly inquiry' that leads to intellectual contributions of various types and not merely publication in refereed discipline based academic journals.
- Business School research must contribute to both core discipline and practice.
- The 'research' should complement the mission of the school.
- The schools must be able to measure the impact of research on targeted audiences.

Consistent with AACSB taskforce report, Darden School of Business decided to undertake 'scholarly inquiry' as an activity to include.

- Formal research by faculty that gets published
- Books and articles written for the benefit of practitioners
- Teaching materials (case studies, simulations, games etc.)
- Pedagogical research (assist others in case method teaching)
- Consulting by faculty (assist practitioners)

Though the above discussion concerning research generally revolves round American Business Schools, there is every reason for Indian business schools to benchmark them in the same way it is done in all the other aspects of management education. Professor Shyam Sundar's (Yale School of Management) commentary on 'Building Research Culture' (China Journal of Accounting Research Vol 1 Issue 1 2008; http://ssrn.com/abstract=1332003) brings out some interesting issues on research culture of business school faculty in Asian Countries.

- Publication in international journals as criteria for promotion and rewards
- Publication of inhouse journals by some universities to disseminate the work of their own faculty without external evaluation of quality
- Objective evaluation of the research by renowned external scholars is highly essential to spot real research talent
- It is not possible to accommodate large quantum of research emanating from Asian giants like China and India in journals of US and Europe, due to space constraints and there is a need to devise inhouse solutions.
- International journals generally publish research that addresses the economies in which their readers reside and research from Asian countries score low on this parameter.
- When Asian faculty addresses the above issue by making their research, reader oriented, it would be at the cost of the problems back in the home economy and no society specially a developing one like India would appreciate it.
- Culture of research in most of the Asian Universities is hierarchy oriented where older lot hold the veto power in acceptance of innovative and new ideas of younger generation. Interpersonal relationships play a major role in developing research culture in Asia.

The eminent professor suggests few simple steps to promote research culture among faculty.

- People holding senior positions should have scholarly accomplishments comparable with the best in the world
- Limiting the power of hierarchy and rank over the creative younger faculty more so when those in authority are not good researchers themselves
- Encourage innovative ideas of younger faculty
- Start radically new journals
- Faculty exchange with good research institutions at minimal costs
- Linking rewards, promotion and tenure to quality research output

Having discussed at length about research, its salient features and importance in business schools, it is imperative to deal with the practical measures that can be adopted at institutional head level to inculcate a sense of research and promote research culture among the faculty. This assumes all the more significance as undertaking Ph.D. or post Ph.D. program is an onerous task that calls for a high level motivation to start with, because research is one activity which cannot be forced down the throat. One has to be motivated enough and thoroughly inspired to take up research. Opined Linda Livingstone, Dean of Graziadio School of Business Pepperdine University. "It is very demanding to get a Ph.D. It takes a number of years to complete and there is a tremendous number of people who start Ph.Ds. they never finish. It's certainly not an issue that will quickly be resolved; it's going to take the work of a lot of people to address the issue over a long period of time."

One of the fundamental objectives of any institutions of higher education is to create knowledge (apart from disseminating it) and this is possible only through research. The fact that the knowledge so created will be useful to the society is a strong motivating force by itself for the faculty to take up research. To echo the words of Linda Livingstone there will be many occasions during the process of carrying out research when the research scholar gets frustrated and feels like leaving it half way through. It is at these critical junctures that the faculty needs 'hand holding' by his learned superiors and the school head. Also many faculty members tend to remain satisfied with a comfortable teaching role doing the same job day in and day out. Not a slide gets changed in their presentations over the years nor any fresh inputs from a journal, magazine or a newly released book find their way into the classroom. Though this situation is more common in the university system, for certain obvious reasons, nothing much could be written home about the business schools in the private sector too who do not lay adequate emphasis on 'faculty research and publication'. Then there are others in the faculty who are not familiar with statistical analysis and language skills to write an interesting research paper or thesis. Yet another aspect is the inability of a faculty to transform a paper presented in a conference into a publishable article in a refereed journal for which one needs to be guided on the nuances involved. This is where motivation and inspiration play a major role.

Mak Khojasteh and Robert A Herring III of Department of Business Administration and Economics, School of Business and Economics, Winston Salem State University, in their paper 'Motivation of Business School Faculty to Conduct Research' suggest a model for motivating faculty to perform research. The primary factors of the model are of particular interest here.

- ***Self fulfilling Prophecy – SFP or "Pygmalion Effect"*** – is defined as a rise in one's effort and consequently performance, in response to another individual's expectation of that particular person (Rothchild 1997). This concept suggests that for example A's expectation for B will cause A to treat B differently, and consequently B will respond in such a way that conforms to A's expectations (Madon S, Jussim L and Eccles J 1994). This principle can be applied by either departmental or school head to set high standards and allocate rewards for achieving them.

- The consequent increase in one's performance can lead to what is called *Perceived Self-Efficacy (PSE)* which is defined as one's belief in one's ability to perform a certain task. Wood and Bandura (1989) stated that "self efficacy refers to beliefs in one's capabilities to mobilise the motivation, cognitive resources and courses of action needed to meet given 'situational demands'". Studies indicate that there is a positive co-relation between PSE and faculty's performance which includes research productivity too (Gist & Mitchell 1992).
- ***Social Capital and Intellectual Capital*: A good interpersonal relation with colleagues characterized by trust, recognition and support constitutes social capital while intellectual capital is the knowledge itself and creation of more knowledge. Both these capitals play a vital role in furthering the research interests of a faculty.

Now to summarize the entire chapter and to convert the whole discussion into a simple set of practical measures that could be considered to be put in place by any business school desirous of promoting serious and active research culture among their faculty.

- Drive home the point that Ph.D. is not the sole prerogative of the select few only
- Make humble beginnings with in house 'newsletters' (print or electronic) and encourage faculty to write (every long journey begins with a small step). Graduate into publishing magazines, journals, edited or self-authored books.
- Constitute a 'research committee' (departmentally as discussed in Chapter 4) consisting of doctoral faculty who could act as reviewers, guides and mentors to young researchers. A research aptitude test could be administered to the aspiring researchers and short-comings addressed.
- Encourage post-doctoral research across disciplines.

- Every senior academician should not only be of scholarly background but continue to engage themselves in further scholarly pursuits to motivate and inspire young researchers. Doctorates generally tend to relax with a feeling of having achieved 'a lot'. Make 'mentorship' compulsory for senior faculty.
- Institute suitable reward and recognition mechanism for those excelling in research and publication.
- Promote case writing and case method of teaching.
- Review lesson plans and presentation material of every course for every semester.
- Lay down achievable targets for faculty for publishing articles, book summaries research papers on quarterly basis and linking them to career growth and incentives.
- Reduce teaching loads, allow flexi hours and provide research associates for those pursuing Ph.D./post Ph.D. programs and grant leave for undertaking fieldwork and survey. A researcher needs uninterrupted time to get into the 'flow' to achieve maximum creativity. Csikszentmihalyi (1990) describes 'flow' as "the state in which people are so involved in an activity that people will do it even at great cost, for the sake of doing it".
- Provide financial support by roping in the industrial houses to sponsor research. Remember research is a time consuming and an expensive activity.
- Make acquiring an M.Phil. or registration into Ph.D. program mandatory for teaching assignments.
- Encourage faculty to pursue research in multiple disciplines like social sciences, liberal arts and environmental sciences etc.
- Provide institutional support in the form of freedom to buy books, access to digital libraries and databases like EBSCO, PROQUEST and EMERALD with wifi broadband Internet

facilities and opportunities to conduct/attend seminars/ conferences at regional/national/ international levels.

- Encourage and even insist on faculty to conduct MDP/ EDPs and to engage in consultancy assignments specially to familiarize 'academic' faculty with the industry working environment.
- Organize 'faculty exchange' programs with institutions known for their research orientation and capabilities.
- Consider starting inhouse Ph.D. programs with external examiners and reviewers.
- Conduct workshops on Statistical Analysis & Techniques, and packages like SPSS and AMOS for the young faculty to aid in their research.
- Insist every department to develop a 'topic or theme bank' for research, consisting of topics which are relevant to business, society or academic and carryout their periodical review.
- Institute regular 'research progress review mechanism' for those pursuing research programs.
- Creation of a 'research culture' where scholarly pursuits are insisted upon and encouraged and where research becomes a way of life and second nature for the faculty.
- Care should be taken to ensure that the success in research does not impair other capabilities of the faculty. 'By the time they earn their degree, doctoral students are generally well prepared as researchers and scholars in their field, but are they similarly prepared for the other faculty roles and responsibility? According to a national survey of doctoral students; probably not.' (Tritelli, 2004, P. 3)

Last but not the least, is the establishment of an exclusive institute to train and turn out Ph.Ds. as is being done by a network of private universities (FedUni) with pan India presence who run one such place quite successfully in Hyderabad basically to meet their own inhouse requirements.

CONSULTANCY

No discussions on research would be complete without touching upon the salient aspects of consultancy by faculty which leads to their professional development and complements their research efforts (Dharni Sinha 2002). Management Consultancy is a key to develop management capability in optimizing all its resources and upgrading efficiency while playing the role of a change agent. One of the objectives of a business school is to contribute to the managerial effectiveness in the industry. Management consultancy provides adequate opportunity to the faculty in ensuring management development of the organization both at individual and at team level. Intellectual offshoot of this process is the self-growth and development of faculty, value addition to his teaching in terms of sharing experiences and complementing the teaching material. In the preface to the book *Consultation*, Blake and Mouton observe 'Consultation and education are two most important influences behind the forward movement of society. In certain respects consultation is even more important than education in giving the society its forward thrust.' The reason is, that consultation alone deals with live ground problems unlike the education where hypothetical academic cases are discussed.

It would be gratifying to note that most global consulting firms have been established by leading management faculty in the United States. There is a positive relationship between consulting, research and teaching effectiveness as per a survey undertaken in the US (1972, 1977) and by Kondrasuk (1981). The experience and knowledge gained in consultancy assignments can be used as useful inputs in teaching and also to train students to look at management consultancy as a career option. Faculty also gains in terms of resolution of industry problems and develop contacts. Academic faculty with no industry exposure would stand to benefit maximum from consultancy. Cascio, John Boudreau, Professor at the Marshall School of Business at the University of Southern California in Los Angeles rightly sums up by saying, 'In my own graduate training, if the professors had not dragged me along to help them with their consulting, I would not have had the advantage of being able to relate to the practice side. It influenced my whole career.'

Though only few top of the rung business schools involve their faculty in consultancy, there is no reason why others should shy away from this intellectually stimulating, professionally challenging and academically beneficial experience for their faculty, not withstanding the commercial interests involved which should not over ride, the former.

Yet another aspect that should not be lost sight of, is the precondition that certain business schools in the private sector place in front of their prospective faculty at the time of recruitment —'to take up consultancy, and EDP for the industry and generate revenue' without laying adequate policy guidelines to that effect. This practice gets more pronounced in cases where certain industrialists form part of either the Board of Management or of the Advisory Council of the School. However, one network of private business schools with pan India presence allows its faculty to claim one-third of the revenue generated through Consultancy/ Executive/ in company training programs as a part of their overall incentive scheme. This has also been highlighted under 'Additional Income Generating Avenues' for the faculty in the chapter that discusses Compensation (Chapter 8).

7
Performance Management

Everyone is bothered about performance, but few seem to be knowing how to measure or manage it.

– Anonymous

Organizations are run and steered by people. Since organizations are collectivities of individuals, the degree of success that individual employees have in reaching the goals set before them is important in determining the organizational effectiveness. The assessment of how successful employees have been at meeting their assigned goals therefore becomes a critical part of human resource management. This leads us to the topic of performance management. Before we go further it is relevant to recapitulate the words of TV Rao who says, *'Performance of an individual in an organizational setting may be defined as the output delivered by an individual in relation to a given role during a particular period of time under the set of circumstances operating at that point of time'.* According to him performance has many dimensions, viz.

- Output or result dimension
- Input dimension
- Time dimension
- Focus dimension
- Quality dimension, and
- Cost dimension

It is through people that goals are set and objectives are realized. The performance of an organization is thus dependant upon the sum total of performance of its members. According to Peter Drucker, 'an organization is like a tune; it is not constituted by individual sounds but by their synthesis'. The success of an organization will therefore depend on its ability to accurately measure the performance of its members and use that measure to objectively optimize or manage their performance.

PERFORMANCE APPRAISAL OR EVALUATION

Performance Appraisal or Evaluation as a system has been in vogue for quite sometime in organizations. There are basically three purposes to which this can be put to use. First it can be used as a basis for rewards allocation. Decisions as to who gets salary increases, promotions and other rewards can be determined. Second, these appraisals can be used for identifying areas where developmental efforts are needed, thus treating it as a major tool for identifying skill and knowledge deficiencies. Finally the performance appraisal can be used as a criterion against which selection devices and developmental programs are validated (Decenzo and Robbins 2003).

Performance appraisal refers to all those procedures that are used to evaluate, the personality, the performance, and the potential of its group members. Evaluation is different from judgment. The former being connected with performance, the latter with person. While evaluation deals with achievement of goals, judgment has an undercurrent of personal attack and is likely to evoke resistance.

The approach to performance management usually incorporates both developmental objectives and reward in business schools. However to some extent both these aspects are compromised by certain constraints which in some cases are beyond the control of institutional heads. The practical experience in this regard is being discussed in the following paragraphs in so far as they relate to business schools.

Performance Appraisal as a system is being replaced by Performance Management a more developmental process rather than an evaluatory one. Certain inherent weaknesses of the appraisal systems are (Townley, 1989):

- More controlling than contributing
- Based on critical review of past performance only, with no opportunity for mid-course corrections
- Rarely linked to organizational needs
- Time consuming and involve laborious paper work
- Undertaken more as an unavoidable evaluatory ritual than as a developmental tool
- Subjectivity may creep in

PERFORMANCE MANAGEMENT

Many people use the term Performance Appraisal interchangeably with Performance Management while the former happens to be one of the major constituents of the latter. Performance Management encompass creativity and managing a work environment or setting in which people are enabled to perform to the best of their abilities. Any effective Performance Management would cover the entire period of a person's tenure in any organization or institution. Such a system should necessarily include the following:

- Development of clear job descriptions
- Proper selection process to ensure person job fit
- Establish requirements and accomplishment based performance standards
- Provide effective orientation, education, training and right environment
- Provide ongoing coaching and feedback ensuring mid course corrections
- Conduct regular performance development interactions
- Design effective reward and recognition systems
- Provide career development and growth opportunities
- Conduct exit interviews and ensure follow-up

Thus it can be seen from the above that Performance Management System (PMS) includes the whole gamut or spectrum of activities starting from job description to the exit interview of an employee, while performance appraisal may only consist of just one or more items listed above. Thus effective performance management system is but an essential feature of a successful organization or an institution.

Similar views were expressed by TV Rao in his write up on 'Implementing Performance Management Systems' even in industries. He opined 'it is very rare to come across a manager who says "we have a good PMS and it is working well". Surveys of fortune 500 or 1000 companies indicate a high degree of dissatisfaction with the performance appraisal systems. This is probably because the nature of performance management is such that it can never elicit a satisfying response from its users or implementers. However, the HR people almost always claim that their PMSs are excellent and working well'. If this is the state of well-organized companies then one can well imagine the status in an educational institution.

Michael Armstrong (2006) describes Performance Management as a self-renewing cycle in which we

- Set the standards in the beginning
- Facilitate and manage performance throughout the year
- Periodically review the performance with a well-designed tool

PERFORMANCE STANDARDS

No performance can be either assessed or measured unless it is made clear to the employee as to what is expected of him/her during the period of review, right in the beginning itself. Performance of a person has to be carefully designed and it cannot be on 'default' basis. Once the standards are set in the beginning of the year, for a faculty to achieve in terms of students' feedback, on his teaching capabilities research and publications, projects, industry interface, institution building and placements of students etc. then at the end of the year all these parameters are measured against the actual achievements of the faculty and his performance assessed too. The rule of the game is "what cannot be measured, cannot be assessed either". Hence it is essential that performance standards for every faculty member are set well before he embarks on the actual performance journey. Like in IBS or in other institutes where written form of student feedback is obtained a faculty is expected to achieve a student feedback rating of 3 on a scale of 5. On publication side a minimum of 4 articles and a research paper are expected annually and a non-doctoral faculty is given four years time to complete his research and obtain Ph.D. Similarly on the industry interface side he is expected to get a minimum of five projects for students, supervise them and assist in their placements too.

Our research has revealed that performance standards are being set in the beginning of the year in about 65 per cent of the business schools surveyed.

TV Rao while studying the PA system of a major corporate (managers and above) observed that managers did not know what was actually expected of them. Managers even went to the extent of saying that 'there is no performance' in their performance appraisal system. From our study, academia appears to have set their house right by formally conveying the performance standards to a faculty member right in the beginning of the review period. All the same a suggested format is attached at Annexure I to this chapter, to improve the system further.

Many organizations use 'SMART' mnemonic to set the standards.

S – Specific and clear objectives
M – Measurable
A – Achievable
R – Relevant to job
T – Timeframe

Students' Feedback

Our research indicates that 80 per cent of the business schools link students' feedback to faculty's actual performance.

Students' feedback on the performance of the faculty is an essential feature of the whole performance management system of the business schools because the student assumes the role of kind of a customer who uses the services rendered by the faculty in seeking the knowledge and skills needed by him. Hence his satisfaction or otherwise is of paramount importance. This becomes much more important when competition is intense among business schools. Few schools don't involve the students in assessing their faculty's performance. One apprehension expressed was that both the parties might misuse the facility and make it more subjective in their own way. Like a faculty may give liberal internal marks to students to get a good feedback and in the process a strict teacher may be rated low, by the students. Yet another important issue is the timing of administering the feedback mechanism. When feedback is taken at the end of the semester/term, the interest levels of the students are generally on the wane which may result in faculty members not getting assessed properly. Two or three evenly spaced feedbacks preferably online through intranet get the faculty his/her actual due. A suggested model for the purpose is placed at Annexure II to this chapter. Caution should be exercised while considering 'too low or too high' feedback by the students, by taking into account the student's attendance, conduct and performance in the class.

The Status

While formal performance appraisals procedures are available, the process of managing and evaluating performance can be informal as well. The formal method involves taking stock of the individual's performance once in a year or so by filling up a specified form and this may or may not involve discussion with the employee. In fact TV Rao in his book *Performance Management* and *Appraisal Systems* (Response Books 2007) argues that specified forms are not important, the objectives, focus, structure and finally implementation are important. Informal methods are assignment oriented, wherein the individual may enjoy a certain degree of functional freedom. Many different methods can be used to gather information about employee performance. However gathering information is only one step in the appraisal process. The information must be evaluated in the organizational context and communicated to employees so that it will result in high levels of performance. Performance management systems are the most logical means to appraise, develop and effectively utilize the knowledge and abilities of employees.

Experience shows that most of the business schools have more or less a laid down appraisal process. In general, the focus is more on the competency assessment than on achievement of any specific goals. Also number of business schools take students' feedback as a part of performance appraisal of the faculty. Students' feedback is taken either at the end of the term in case of a trimester system or on completion of a semester in case of semester pattern of education, while the performance appraisal of the faculty in almost all the cases is resorted to, on annual basis only. Students should be encouraged to give fair and objective feedback without fear or favour (courage of conviction) and care should be taken to ensure that no faculty turns vindictive towards students from whom he receives an unpleasant feedback.

FAIRNESS OF PERFORMANCE APPRAISAL

Performance appraisal should not only be fair but it should also be seen, felt and perceived as fair. Because most of the grievances relate or owe their origin to performance appraisals as human beings have an inherent tendency of comparing themselves with, and always consider themselves to be more talented and more deserving than their colleagues. Hence certain pitfalls whether intended or otherwise generally occur while every effort should be made to make the system error free to the extent possible. Ethics play a vital role in appraising the performance of an employee. McKellogg suggested following do's and dont's which are relevant here.

- Don't appraise without knowing why it is needed
- Appraise on the basis of representative information
- Appraise on the basis of sufficient information
- Be honest in your assessment of all the facts you have obtained
- Don't write one thing and say another
- Make it plain that this is your personal opinion of facts as you see them
- Pass an appraisal information only to those who have good reasons to want it
- Don't imply the existence of appraisal that has not been made
- Don't accept another's appraisal without knowing the basis on which it has been made

Yet another important feature of performance appraisal is that it cannot, rather should not be delegated to anyone. Perhaps this is the only activity that cannot be delegated in the organizations or institutions.

It is encouraging to note that faculty in 70 per cent of the schools surveyed by us feel that their performance appraisal is fair. Nevertheless efforts should be made to bring in the rest 30 per cent also into this fold, in the overall interest of the organization.

PROMOTION POLICY

One of the objectives of performance appraisal system is to assess an employees' suitability to handle higher responsibilities. Promotion is one thing which every employee looks forward to as it fulfills the psychological needs more than what it does to monetary needs. In an organization there would be number of employees who get motivated more by things like recognition and reward, higher job responsibilities in terms of job enlargement/enrichment, higher designation, and certain status linked/perks, etc. than they do by money alone though money still continues to be the single largest motivating factor of all the things for most of the employees. Promotion of an employee makes every one in the family happy and his status in the society gets elevated while the same may not be possible by merely a pay rise.

In business schools, the entry level positions for the faculty are normally at Research Associate (RA), or at Faculty Associate (FA), while some may have Assistant Lecturer and Lecturer, positions. Then they move up the chain to become Faculty Member or Senior Lecturer as the case may be. Next step is the Reader or the Associate Dean, while Dean, Professor or Director are the positions falling next. Some business schools are headed by Deans while heads of certain institutes are known as Directors (IIMs, IBS, etc.) while some have both (IBS) with Director as the head of the institution and Deans heading other functions such as research, administration, academics and exams. Intermediate positions like Senior Faculty Member, Senior Professor, etc. also exist in the hierarchy of academic assignments. However there is no consistency across most of the private business schools and generally every institute has its own norms to recruit faculty at a particular level and move him/her up the hierarchy based on performance. A suggested model of faculty along with necessary eligibility conditions is given at Annexure IV to this chapter, which it is felt would motivate faculty to look forward to higher position if they perform well.

Self-Assessment

A management faculty is a 'knowledge worker' to that extent supposedly a mature, conscientious, and a sincere human being who is generally true to himself. Hence, it is essential that he gets a fair chance to present his own assessment of his performance during the period of review against the performance standards set for him at the beginning of the review period. A suggested format is given at the end of this chapter as Annexure V. This can also be used as an upward communication instrument through which a faculty can convey his professional developmental needs and also offer suggestions if any. The assessing authority can either ratify or reject the self-assessment claims made by the faculty, with or without assigning any reasons which in any case would be taken care of while carrying out appraisal as per Annexure III.

SUMMING UP

Performance appraisal or evaluation or review process dates back to times immemorial (1842 Federal Govt. in USA) when Congress passed a law mandating yearly performance reviews for department clerks, and slowly it spread to all organized activity centres. While it has matured in government and corporates, it is still in a 'nascent stage' in educational institutions. It's time this evaluatory process matures into a developmental one by having a sound Performance Management System (PMS) in place in business schools.

Our research on Performance Appraisal of Faculty in business schools reveals that students' feedback is linked to performance of the faculty while assessing it and that business schools by and large do set performance standards for their faculty at the beginning of the year. Further it was validated statistically that the performance appraisal of the faculty is fair but faculty do not generally get their promotions as per their own turn.

Though the written responses of the faculty were on the positive side but on probing verbally further the actual situation prevailing appeared to be little different and faculty expressed their desire to have the PMS improved in all the areas. In view of the criticality and the sensitivity of the issue, managements of business schools may seriously consider improving the existing systems or introducing ab initio.

Based on our study the following issues concerning performance management were found to be meriting serious attention by business schools.

- The importance of performance management as an essential feature of HRM practices needs no further emphasis as what cannot be managed or measured, cannot be assessed too. There is an increased demand for countability in personal assessment, and evaluation in management education in view of the costs involved. Effective faculty performance management systems are in the best interests of all the stakeholders, i.e. students, faculty, managements, and the industry.

- During our study though outwardly faculty did respond favourably for all questions relating to performance appraisal indicating a general state of satisfaction, but on close probing and assurance of confidentiality, it came to light that there is a vast scope for improvement, in all aspects. Management education would largely benefit if faculty accountability is increased, more so when it is based on a system devised by the faculty themselves. The challenge lies in having a proper system in the first place and then implementing it effectively. A significant outcome of our informal discussions with the faculty on this issue, is the 'lack of transparency' in the sense, the annual assessment/evaluation is not discussed with the faculty concerned. The faculty remains in dark about his weaknesses, and thus makes no efforts to develop himself. The format suggested by us at Annexure III addresses this anamoly where the review process is discussed with the faculty who acknowledges and signs on it.

  Second major issue deals with the formal setting of performance standards in the beginning of the review period. No institution under our study was found to be following this practice though positive responses were obtained from the faculty for a question on this aspect. Yet another issue that cropped up during informal discussions is the lack of promotional avenues for management faculty. A change in the designation every three or four years with associate benefits (however small they may be) would go a long way in boosting the morale of the faculty and they would be motivated to give their best.

- Suggested formats for setting performance standards, self-assessment, faculty annual review, for obtaining student feedback, and creating a hierarchy model for promotions are given at Annexures I to V to this chapter which may help institutional heads to formulate their own methods depending upon the operating circumstances. Care has been taken to keep the review formats as simple as possible so that the assessing/reviewing authorities do not tend to treat the 'review process' as an unavoidable and a monotonous ritual.

FOOD FOR THOUGHT

The quality expert W Edwards Deming had a different take on performance evaluation/appraisal systems (Human Resources Management: John M. Ivancevich Tata McGraw-Hill 2003 – P. 259). As per him the flaws in the performance appraisal systems are:

- Short-term performance focused
- Deflect attention from long-term planning
- Ratees are generally disappointed
- Resists creativity and divergence in views
- Tend to foster politics, and groupism
- More number crunching and less actual measurement of the performance
- Focus more on 'result' and less on 'process' and 'quality'.
- Cause concern, fear and stress in the minds of the ratees
- Tend to be more judgmental rather than being developmental.

In the light of above criticism which almost amounts to serious indictment of the existing systems/formats, please examine each format in use in your establishment and suggest methods to improve them so that none of them suffers from the above mentioned anomalies.

Annexure I

ABC Business School
(Department of ....)

Date: ....

To
Prof: ....
Designation: ....

Dear Prof

Performance Standards for a Faculty Member

1. Your performance review period starts on .... and ends on ....
2. You are expected to ensure the following minimum performance standards during the above period of review.
   - Teach a minimum of .... Courses/term/semester/year
   - Earn a minimum student feedback of .... on a scale of ....
   - Publish — Number
     - Magazine articles/cases –
     - Book reviews/summaries –
     - Research papers –
       (National/International Journals) –
   - Present Papers in
     - Local/regional seminars –
     - National Seminars –
     - International conferences –
   - Industry Interface
     - Organize guest lectures –
     - Arrange projects for students –

    - Supervise/guide students' projects –
    - Arrange placements for students
    - Take up consultancy assignment –
- Institutional Image Building
    - Edit a newsletter/magazine/journal –
    - Organize seminars/conferences –
    - Organize media coverage –
    - Build up intellectual resources –

3. Take up Doctoral Program/Post-Doctoral Program and complete the same in .... years time.
4. All the above are intended to serve as guidelines only and your proactive approach and innovative ideas to add value to students and to the institution will always be welcome.
5. Kindly sign on the duplicate copy and return it to us as a token of your acknowledgement.
6. Wishing you all the very best in all your endeavours.

Yours Sincerely

XYZ ....
HOD (Dept of ....)

Annexure II

Suggested Format for Feedback on Faculty by Students

			Teaching Skills					Professional Characteristics					Total
S.N.	Faculty name	Course taught	Sound subject knowledge	Coverage of syllabus	Strong communica-tion presentation and active listening	Example & case discussion	Evaluation method used	Organization and classroom mgt.	Creative interesting & imaginative	Fair with an inclusive respectful approach	Good rapport & empathy	Relationship with students monitoring skills	* All ave's/avg.

Note: Scale of rating and minimum standard to be achieved by a faculty may be decided by the management.

Annexure III

Faculty Annual Review and Development Report

For the Academic Year/Period ....

Emp. Code: .... Name of Faculty Member: ....

Department: .... Designation: ....

Assessment is to be done in the light of performance standards set, and the self-assessment form submitted by the faculty. It is the performance that is to be reviewed and not the person per se. Developmental Aspects are not to be lost sight of.

Grading as per Self-Assessment By Faculty

1. Your assessment of the faculty member: (Tick one)

   A. Teaching Capabilities & Subject knowledge

      ❐ Outstanding ❐ Excellent ❐ Good
      ❐ Satisfactory ❐ Unsatisfactory ☐

   B. Student Interface & Classroom Management

      ❐ Outstanding ❐ Excellent ❐ Good
      ❐ Satisfactory ❐ Unsatisfactory ☐

   C. Research & Intellectual Capabilities

      ❐ Outstanding ❐ Excellent ❐ Good
      ❐ Satisfactory ❐ Unsatisfactory ☐

   D. Industry Interface

      ❐ Outstanding ❐ Excellent ❐ Good
      ❐ Satisfactory ❐ Unsatisfactory ☐

   E. Institution Building

      ❐ Outstanding ❐ Excellent ❐ Good
      ❐ Satisfactory ❐ Unsatisfactory ☐

F. Personal Attributes and Team Player Attributes

❒ Outstanding ❒ Excellent ❒ Good
❒ Satisfactory ❒ Unsatisfactory

G. Overall Grading

❒ Outstanding ❒ Excellent ❒ Good
❒ Satisfactory ❒ Unsatisfactory

2. Detailed remarks (To highlight strong and weak points needing special mention)

   E.g.: Strong Point: *A motivational speaker or an inspiring personality*
   Weak Point: *Lack of cross-functional business knowledge*

3. Developmental measures suggested

   E.g.: • *To improve cross-functional business knowledge*
   • *To be more interactive in the class*

....

Signature of the Faculty

4. Recommendations

   (Not to be disclosed to faculty)

   May include promotion/demotion, pay hike/no hike, confirmation or extension or probation, or training abroad, etc.

....

Signature of Assessing Authority

---

5. (Remarks of the reviewing Authority)

   I do/do not concur with the above (score out 'not applicable') ....

   ....

   ....

School Head

(Paras 4 and 5 are to be filled up after discussing the review process with the faculty and obtaining his signatures)

Annexure IV

Suggested Hierarchy Model and Promotion Criteria in a Typical Business School

Designation		Recommended Eligibility
• Research Associate (RA)/ Junior Lecturer/Teaching Assistant (TA)	:	MBAs with minimum two years work experience and academic bent of mind: To be put as Understudy to a Faculty
• Faculty Associate (FA)/ Lecturer	:	Two years as RA/Junior Lecturer/TA (starts actual teaching)
• Faculty Member/ Senior Lecturer	:	Two years as FA/Lecturer
• Senior Faculty Member/ Assistant Professor	:	Three years as FM/Senior Lecturer
• Associate Professor/ Reader/Associate Dean	:	Three years as SFM/Assistant Professor
• Professor/Deputy Dean	:	Three years as Associate Dean/Prof./ Reader and Ph.D.
• Senior Professor/Dean/ HOD	:	Three years as Professor or Deputy Dean
• Director	:	Five years as Senior Professor or Dean/HOD or twenty years of teaching experience with a Ph.D.

Note: Designation and eligibility conditions may be altered for candidates with exceptional qualifications and experience both in academics and industry depending upon the individual merits. As a general guideline, a consistent performance for a period of three years may be considered essential for promotion to next level.

Annexure V

Self-Assessment by Faculty

For the period from .... to ....

(To be read in reference to Performance Standards set on ....)

Name of the Faculty: ....

Department: ....

Designation: .... Date of Joining: ....

In pursuance of the performance standards set for me vide Department of .... letter dated .... I assess my performance during the period from .... to .... as under.

1. Self-Developmental Activities undertaken during the review period. (like additional qualifications acquired or projects undertaken, etc.)

2. I achieved all the performance standards set for me.

   Or

   I could not achieve all the performance standards set for me and the shortfalls with the reasons thereof are mentioned below.

   Or

   I exceeded the performance standards set for me the details of which are given below. (additional achievements only) (score 'out not applicable').

3. I rate myself as under (Outstanding – O, Excellent – E, Good – G, Satisfactory – S, Unsatisfactory – US). (Use abbreviations)

- Teaching Capabilities and Subject Knowledge ☐
- Student Interface and Classroom Management ☐
- Research and Intellectual Capabilities ☐
- Industry Interface ☐
- Institution Building ☐
- Personal Attributes ☐
- Overall Grading ☐

4. I request for the following professional development facilities.

5. I have the following suggestions to make.

Date: ....

Place: Signature of the Faculty

....

Remarks by the Assessing Authority

I do/do not concur with the above self-assessment (score out 'not applicable').

....

Signature of the Assessing Authority

8

Compensation

Do your job and demand compensation – but in that order.

– Cary Grant

Michael Armstrong and Helen Murlis define reward management as 'reward management is concerned with the formulation and implementation of strategies and policies that aim to reward people fairly, equitably and consistently in accordance with their value to the organization. It deals with the design, implementation and maintenance of reward process and practices that are geared to the improvement of organizational, team and individual performance.' Rosabeth Moss Kanter of Harvard says of reward management as 'when people have the opportunity to act on their own initiative to shape their own work and feel they are rewarded for making a difference, they can do great things – that's been true throughout the ages'.

Compensation is what employees receive in exchange for their contribution to the organization. Employees exchange their work, in return for monetary and non-monetary gratification. Money is considered the most important gratifier and source of motivation for employees, although non-financial incentives also play a significant role. Modern work theory suggests that

- Money is a major element in any effective total reward system.
- Salaries and wages are widely considered as 'merit badges'. They are status symbols.
- Non-financial rewards may appeal to some and are cheaper.

- Levels of commitment and effort promised by non-financial rewards could be bought with money only at prohibitive cost.

The above theory indicates that an ideal employer has to have a keen sense of empathy, and must decide how to balance and combine money rewards and non-monetary rewards and to learn what combination of rewards will provide the biggest pay offs.

The strategic aim of compensation management is to develop and implement relevant policies and processes to support the achievement of organizational goals. These aims could be listed as:

- Reward people for their value addition/contribution
- Reward processes to be based on values and beliefs of the organization.
- Reward differentially for the different outputs of people
- Reward to attract and retain right people for right jobs
- Reward to enhance performance of people
- Reward to develop and nurture relationships
- Reward to achieve the goals of the organization

In *Treat People Right* Ed Lawler stresses the importance of creating a 'virtuous spiral' in which both employers and employees win. He identifies a number of principles for achieving this, which look at the whole HRM agenda from creating the right value proposition on recruitment through to quality of leadership. He states that 'it is entirely possible to design a reward system that motivates people to work and satisfies them while at the same time contributing to organizational effectiveness'.

Strategic Compensation Planning is the compensation of employees in ways that enhance motivation and growth while at the same time aligning their efforts with the objectives, philosophies and culture of the organization. It has three important aspects: linking compensation to organizational objectives, the pay for performance standard and motivating employees through compensation.

Employee compensation is a central part of the employment relationship and an employee considers it as a measure of success. Therefore, it becomes crucial for any organization to carefully manage the compensation related issues. Thus there is a strong need for a systematic and consistent approach for measuring and recording the relative worth of a job and consequently that of an employee performing it. All the definitions of compensation management given by the experts point to one common thing, i.e. the reward system must satisfy and motivate people to work and put in their best to contribute to organizational success and effectiveness.

COMPENSATION OF MANAGEMENT FACULTY

Without adequate compensation, current employees are likely to leave the organization and the newer ones will hesitate to join. 'Bad pay master' is a term coined to refer to poorly paying organizations. Also pay dissatisfaction affects quality of work and work life and also triggers grievances. Teaching in our country unfortunately is not a very popular profession and is, traditionally and historically slightly looked down upon. Hence very few take up this job and that also as the last resort. The main reason for this state of affairs is the poor pay and the status associated with the profession. A proverb in Telugu language says 'if you cannot survive otherwise, then become a teacher'. This age old attitude of the society and the government, percolated to all levels of education system say from KG to PG. Fortunately business schools are better off in this regard though a lot is still to be done there too.

To apply the above aspects to the pay of a management faculty, it is necessary to first identify the objectives of the business school say in terms of quality students output, their absorption in the quality jobs and subsequently, their quality performance on the job.

A faculty or a group of faculty who can ensure the above objectives can have their compensation linked accordingly.

Relevant information can be obtained through students' feedback and feedback from the industry. Next is the 'pay for performance standard' under which an optimum level of performance standard is set. For example, in a particular business school system, a faculty is expected to teach three courses in a trimester or a semester and obtain a student feedback of 3 on a scale of 5. Additional courses handled by the faculty are compensated separately. Similarly exemplary student feedback makes him eligible for 'best teacher' award. Interestingly productivity studies show that employees increase their output by 15 to 35 per cent when an organization installs a pay for performance program. Compensation is also a major motivational tool for employees. Motivated they will be only when 'pay equity' is achieved or when they feel that the compensation they received is equal to the value of work performed. Research clearly demonstrates that employees' perception of pay equity or inequity can have dramatic effects on their motivation for both work behaviour and productivity. This is further authenticated by the expectancy theory of motivation which predicts that one's level of motivation depends on the attractiveness of the rewards sought and the probability of obtaining those rewards. Some managements may also resort to 'pay secrecy' practices where one faculty does not know what his colleague is getting. Above mentioned business school network for instance is following this practice. This secrecy serves to cover up inequities existing within the internal pay structure, though the downside is, it may lead employees to believe that there is no direct relationship between pay and performance. Management faculty gets salaries and incentives either as per AICTE, or UGC scales or a combination, or on adhoc basis, (consolidated) or on market driven basis. It is a well known fact that a management faculty gets much lower salary than what his own freshly graduating student gets outside in the industry.

RESEARCH ANALYSIS

Research was carried out prior to revision of AICTE or UGC pay scales and the analysis on compensation of faculty in business schools revealed that

- 40 per cent business schools offer AICTE pay scales, 24 per cent pay UGC scales and the remaining have adhoc pay structures.
- 60 per cent faculty are not satisfied with their compensation and are not rewarded for their exemplary performance.
- Incentive systems are existing only in 50 per cent business schools.

Total Reward Approach *(Michael Armstrong 2006)*

Total reward is the combination of financial and non-financial rewards available to employees while 'total remuneration' is the value of all cash payments and benefits received by them. A 'reward strategy' needs to be formulated in every business school based on the following factors:

- Job evaluation
- Market rates
- Basic pay structure for the grade
- Special pay or variable pay if any
- Employee benefits
- Allowances
- Incentives

All the above constitute what we call as 'transactional rewards' while the 'relational awards' contain the following:

- Providing necessary facilities for learning and development.
- Ensuring career progression based on performance.
- Creating a conducive work environment where talent is recognized and rewarded, work–life balance is ensured, upward communication is facilitated and sound leadership is more than assured.

Thus the most powerful argument to the above mentioned total reward approach was made by Pfeffer (1998) as

Creating a fun, challenging and empowered work environment, in which individuals are able to use their abilities to do meaningful jobs for which they are shown appreciation, is likely to be a more certain way to enhance motivation and performance – even though creating such an environment may be more difficult and take more time than simply turning the reward lever.

Let us now discuss various components that form part of 'transactional rewards' with the assumption that 'relational rewards' would be adequately taken care of, by every business school head.

Scales or Grades of Pay

Poorly compensated jobs lead to absenteeism and other forms of employee withdrawal too. Even over payment can harm the organization and its people causing anxiety, guilt and discomfort. Over the years, aspirations for a better quality of life, employee expectations on benefits and facilities have increased substantially. The initial approach to minimize benefits and pay poorly and then let the employee deal with his own problems or needs has undergone a significant change with the steep rise in demand for management education.

Compensation for Efforts

Pay constitutes a quantitative measure of an employee's relative worth. For most employees pay has a direct bearing not only on their standard of living but also on the status and recognition they may be able to achieve both on and off the job. Since pay represents a reward received in exchange for an employee's contributions, it is essential, according to equity theory that the pay be equitable in terms of those contributions. It is essential also that an employee's pay be equitable in terms of what other employees are receiving for their contributions. Equity theory also referred as 'distributive fairness' is a motivation theory that explains how people respond to situations in which they feel they have received less (or more) than they deserve. Central to the theory is the role of perception in motivation and the fact that individuals make comparisons. It states that individuals form a ratio of their inputs (abilities, skills and experiences) in a situation to their outcomes (salary, benefits) in that situation. They then compare the value of that ratio with the value of the input/output ratio for other individuals in a similar class of jobs either internal or external to the organization. If the value of their ratio equals the value of another's, they perceive the situation as equitable and no tension exists. However, if they perceive their input/output ratio as inequitable relative to others, this creates tension and forces them to eliminate or reduce the inequity. As a thumb rule either AICTE or UGC Pay scales (revised in the year 2009 and accepted by most of the States) could be considered for implementation with suitable modifications where found necessary. The decision to hire a person at a particular pay band is a sensitive one and adequate care needs to be exercised.

Special or Variable Pay

This could be considered for the faculty who discharge additional responsibilities (administrative or otherwise) over and above their teaching assignments. These duties include, hostel warden, student counselor, student services head, academic co-ordinator, controller of examinations consulting editor of newsletter/magazine or a journal (published by the school). The recently introduced Grade Pay (GP) in AICTE and UGC scales could also form part of this.

Employee Benefits

The following could constitute employee benefits

- Leave (casual, earned, sick leave with half/full/no pay)
- Contributory provident fund and pension fund
- Gratuity
- Leave encashment facility
- Medical allowance and healthcare insurance

- Conveyance allowance
- Leave travel concession or allowance
- Any other benefit as deemed suitable

Allowances

Following may be considered

- Dearness allowance at appropriate rates and linked to CPI (Consumer Price Index)
- City Compensatory Allowance (CCA)
- House Rent Allowance (HRA) where 'in campus' housing is not provided
- Magazine/periodicals allowance
- Research allowance (post- and pre-doctoral)

INCENTIVES

A clear trend in strategic compensation management is the growth of incentive plans. Incentive rewards are based entirely upon a 'pay for performance' philosophy. Incentive pay programs establish a performance 'threshold' (a base line performance level) that an employee must reach in order to qualify for incentive payments. Additionally incentive plans emphasize a shared focus on organizational objectives by broadening the opportunities for incentives to employees. Incentive plans create working environment that promotes a philosophy of commitment and passion through the belief that every individual contributes to organizational effectiveness.

Every employee looks forward to be rewarded for doing work or extra work and management faculty are no exception to this basic tenet of working life. Some of the functional areas where a faculty deserves to be rewarded for doing that extra but a vital bit are:

- Research, pre- or post-doctoral
- Publication (Books—Derivative or Self-Authored/Research Papers/Articles)

- Presentation of Papers in various seminars/conferences
- On being selected as 'Best Teacher' for the term/semester/year
- Maintaining industry interface through projects and placements for students
- Undertaking consultancy and executive training assignments
- Referring new faculty members into the system
- 'Loyalty Incentive', for long service (more than 3, 5, 8 and 10 years in a row)
- Teaching courses over and above the specified load
- Taking on assignments like Controller of Examinations, Academic Co-ordinator and Projects Co-ordinator in addition to normal teaching load.
- Question paper setting and answer book evaluation
- For conducting seminars/conferences
- For any other 'value adding activity' as deemed fit by the Head of the institution.

For an incentive plan to be successful employees must be able to see a clear connection between the incentive payments they receive and their job performance. Managements should never allow incentive payments to be seen as an 'entitlement'. Instead these payments should be viewed as a reward that must be earned through effort. This perception can be strengthened if the incentive money is distributed to employees in a separate cheque. This is practiced in one of the well known business schools chains wherein faculty are paid incentives for various activities listed above. Incentives could be in the form of cash or even kind where a faculty member's ward can undergo free education in the very institute where the faculty member is serving. A very famous business school in the country offers free MBA program by waiving the entire tuition fee to the wards of their employees who have put in five years of service in the school and continue to serve the organization.

ADDITIONAL INCOME GENERATING AVENUES

In addition to all the statutory and non-statutory compensation benefits, business schools can go ahead and create further avenues for the talented faculty to generate additional income (In premier business schools faculty make more money through consultancy assignments than their regular pay and allowances).

These could be in the form of

- Consultancy assignments
- EDP/MDPs
- Project work
- Faculty referral schemes
- Handling additional teaching loads
- Course material preparation
- Case writing
- Edited (Derivative) or self-authored books publication
- Taking on administrative responsibilities
- Marketing of programs and publications of the school

SUMMING UP

Compensation must reward employees for past efforts (pay for performance) while serving to motivate employees' future performance. The basis on which compensation payments are determined and the way they are administered, can significantly effect employee productivity and the achievement of organizational goals. Similarly the success of an incentive pay plan depends on the organizational climate in which it operates, employees' confidence in it and its suitability to employees' and organizational needs.

On the whole it can be gauged from our study that there is a widespread dissatisfaction among the faculty about their compensation, rewards and incentive systems which was also corroborated by the faculty and the institutional heads during the personal interactions of the researcher with them.

Since there is a considerable improvement in AICTE and UGC pay scales revised in the year 2009, the solution lies in making sure all institutes in the private sector grant their faculty members AICTE pay scales or UGC scales and link the Dearness Allowance (DA) to theConsumer Price Index (CPI) so that whenever government announces rise in the DA rates (as a % of the basic salary), the same benefit also accrues to the faculty members. In addition there is a dire need to institute an effective incentive mechanism in business schools to motivate the faculty to give their best.

CASE STUDY

NEITHER PAY NOR PROMOTION

Background

Prof Joshi joined Competent School of Management Nagpur in the year 2000 with a basic pay of ₹12000 pm along with all other statutory allowances at central government rates. Apart from teaching HR courses he also starts handling academic co-ordination, general administration and students' services etc. on proactive basis as students are his first love and no one else was there to perform these duties. Later in the year Mr. Kapoor, an IIM alumni with lot of industry experience, joins as faculty member in the finance stream. Few months down the line, the Dean, Mr. Vengaskar, one fine afternoon is handed the pink slip for spending more time on 'trading' than on teaching or running the institution. Moves in Mr. Kapoor as the new Dean and Prof Joshi also gets rewarded in terms of getting promoted as Associate Professor and his basic pay goes up to ₹14500 pm. Both Kapoor and Joshi in the next three years take the school to greater heights and it becomes very popular in Western India achieving a very high rank among private business schools of the area, in the ranking surveys conducted by well known business presses. During this period, number of new faculty members are absorbed with pay reportedly better than that of Prof Joshi. By then the school also starts the system of 'Pay Secrecy' wherein no one including the head of the institution gets to know the compensation details of a newly recruited faculty member. But somehow people manage to get to know such things. The school also has a policy of giving promotion and pay rise to faculty members who perform well consecutively for three years.

The Situation

Not withstanding the better pay packets given to the newly inducted faculty, Prof Joshi waits for his turn for promotion and pay rise at the end of three years in the present position. Moment of truth comes in when Prof Kapoor gets promoted as Director with improved pay and perks while Prof Joshi is left high and dry in the same position though with a marginal rise of ₹900 pm in all. Prof Joshi is a demoralized man today.

POINTS FOR DISCUSSION

1. Do you think the 'Compensation Policy' of the school is fair? If so or if not, why?
2. What is your concept of 'Pay Parity'?
3. Do you feel Prof Joshi is rewarded adequately for his performance?
4. What would you do if you are in the position of either Prof Joshi and of Prof Kapoor? Justify your actions.
5. Pay 'Secrecy or Transparency', which is better and why?
6. What effective measures do you suggest in the 'compensation and reward policy' of a business school so as to avoid recurrence of Prof Joshi's cases?

9
Morale, Motivation and Organizational Climate

The best morale exist when you never hear the word mentioned. When you hear a lot of talk about it, it's usually lousy.

– D.D. Eisenhower

MORALE

No matter how well paid and interesting jobs are, if the people performing them do not get on well together and respect each other's abilities then morale will be adversely affected. In fact these days, the interpersonal relationships between the employees is assumed to constitute what is called the 'social capital' of the organization in addition to the existing physical (infrastructural) and financial capitals. Morale is closely linked to motivation. If the employees are highly motivated to do what they are expected to, and they enjoy every bit of it, then the morale of employees is assumed to be sound and high.

The state of morale in any business organization can be judged by the degree of willingness its employees show towards their work. Satisfaction at work is the principal indicator of high morale which in a way means that pay must represent a fair reward, the duties of the job must hold the employee's interest and above all he must enjoy the social contacts established at his workplace. Every organization is a sum of individuals whose morale depends on their mutual adjustments and interpersonal relationships. If this is satisfactory, new comers will be readily accepted into the fold. It is the manager's social skill in creating an effective team spirit among his subordinates that helps in building sound morale in the organization, as the link between morale and other aspects of HRM is very strong. This is irrespective of the type of organization, be it commercial or education. Certain measures that contribute to improving the morale in a business school are:

- Right man for the right job and providing role clarity
- Equal pay and equal opportunities
- Open communication in all matters both academic and administrative
- Reward and recognition of merit
- Foster teamwork
- Frequent social interactions to develop family like culture
- Consultative approach in dealing with problems and taking decisions
- Gradual introduction of changes if any
- Paying attention to the personal problems of faculty and solving them to the extent possible
- Head of the institution to be in continuous touch with the faculty both on and off the work

Sound morale leads to self-discipline among the faculty with regard to punctuality and adherence to rules and regulations of the institute. This is a very important issue since the students very closely observe their faculty members, any bad form of conduct, by the faculty may prove detrimental to the 'role model' image, he or she is expected to maintain.

MOTIVATION

People often say that motivation does not last.
Well, neither does bathing – that's why we recommend it daily.

– Zig Ziglar

The most fundamental principle of human motivation is that people are motivated by self interest. This principle is referred to as 'what's in it for me' or WIIFM. Before working hard to accomplish a task one would like to know how one would benefit from it. Similarly if a faculty is asked to prepare a research paper he might be motivated to work up to the best of his ability. But before actually getting down to the task he would go through the WIIFM exercise. To motivate people using the WIIFM principle, one needs to be aware of the intensity of a person's desire. A person can be highly motivated, mildly motivated, or only slightly motivated, depending upon intensity of his or her own WIIFM principle. In simple terms, responding to the needs of the people is called motivation. These needs could be psychological (recognition hungry) or physical (craving for money and comforts). Studies indicate that 99 per cent of employees are motivated by one or more of the following seven needs and if satisfied consequently their morale also would be high

- Needs for achievement
- Needs for power
- Needs for affiliation
- Needs for autonomy
- Needs for esteem
- Needs for safety and security
- Needs for equity

An attempt is generally made in the organizations to change behaviour (Behaviour Modification) through rewards and punishments, because human beings by nature tend to repeat behaviour that leads to a positive consequence and avoid the one that leads to negative consequence (Law of effect).

QUALITY OF WORK

Quality and beauty are more difficult to define as to what they really are rather than what they are not. A cliché, 'quality is a long and neverending journey and not a destination' is a more appropriate definition which implies scope for Continuous Improvement (CI-kaizen). However the International Organization for Standardization (ISO) defines quality as "the totality of characteristics of an entity that bears on its ability to satisfy stated and implied needs".

Management faculty members are concerned with imparting quality education to students. Any student will have learning objectives in the form of seeking knowledge, acquiring skills, an ability to differentiate and finally developing own character so as to become a useful member of the society. Quality education is something that guarantees a student all the above mentioned four objectives, and by building attractive features into; it also makes the learning process a joy for the student.

Academic quality is the quantum of learning opportunities provided to the student to gain an academic award or a degree or a diploma. These opportunities are in the form of effective teaching, administrative support and proper assessment, internship and projects, industrial visits, independent assignments, seminars, workshops, role plays, counseling and mentoring, etc.

Next thing is, adherence to quality norms in turning out an appreciable product is a joyful and highly motivating experience for an employee. It is a highly gratifying experience for a teacher to have delivered a quality presentation. Most of the teachers restrict themselves to imparting knowledge and skills only to the students and rarely attend to personality development needs of the student. The reasons could be, low morale and motivational levels caused by various factors like less pay, lack of supervision and even recognition of good work, etc. If only a teacher is convinced of the role he plays in adding value to the student in particular and thereby to the whole nation in general he/she would definitely do his/her best.

The solution lies in management attending to these motivational needs of the faculty and initiating suitable measures.

It is only when an employee is very happy in his organization that he tends to get his friends inducted into the organization. This is what we call recruitment through employee reference.

ORGANIZATIONAL CLIMATE

Organizational climate refers to the 'perceptions that organization members share, of fundamental elements of their organization'. Moran and Volkwein (1992) defined organizational climate as a relatively enduring characteristic of an organization, which distinguishes it from other organization, further it: (a) embodies members collective perceptions about their organization with respect to such dimensions as autonomy, trust, cohesiveness, support, recognition, innovation and fairness; (b) is produced by member interactions; (c) serves as a basis for interpreting and responding to the situation; (d) reflects the prevalent norms and attitudes of the organizations culture, and (e) acts as a source of influence for sharing behaviour.

Burke and Litwin (1992) define climate in terms of perceptions that individuals have of, how their local work unit is managed and how effectively they and their day-to-day colleagues work together on the job. Climate and culture are related but not the same. Climate is much more in the foreground of organizational members' perceptions, whereas culture is more in the background and defined by beliefs and values. Climate is affected by culture and peoples' perceptions define both but at different levels.

ORGANIZATIONAL CLIMATE IN AN EDUCATIONAL ENTERPRISE

Research in the area of organizational climate was greatly facilitated by the development of the Organizational Climate Description Questionnaire (OCDQ) by Halpin and Croft in 1963 as it relates to educational enterprise. These mainly involve various behavioural dimensions at the institutional head level as to how *supportive, directive, restrictive, collegial, intimate and disengaged* they are. It has been established that characteristics of 'social needs' are very important for co-operative staff endeavours. Feeling of sense of accomplishment is yet another need of the faculty to promote positive organizational culture/climate. Moreover on an open climate no one needs to supervise or monitor another as everyone goes about doing his job with passion. Hoy Smith and Sweet Land (2002) developed an Organizational Climate Index (OCI) which has four dimensions such as: Collegial Leadership (CL); Professional Teacher Behaviour (PTB); Achievement Press (AP) and Institutional Vulnerability (IV) etc.

Management students are mature adults with an average age of 23-24 years and some of them have work experience of 2 to 5 years, and they would like to be treated as such. Any rigour in the form of strict discipline is likely to be resented. An informal and friendly learning environment is what they normally look forward to. Thus faculty is required to be responsive to such needs of the students and managements in turn have to provide that kind of environment in their institutions. Like a faculty must feel happy to come to the office everyday and so should he at the end of the day and he or she should willingly participate in all the social functions or get-togethers of the institution preferably with their spouses. This will bring a kind of 'family culture' to the institution and sense of ownership and belongingness increase as the days pass by. Also a management student expects the faculty to be available to him as and when he needs the guidance irrespective of the day and time. No doubt all the premier business schools like IIMs and others have fully residential campuses where students stay in the hostels and faculty live in their quarters within the campus. Though informal organizational climate does not mean throwing the rule book away, but creating a friendly environment where teaching and learning become joyful experiences, within the framework of basic rules and regulations. No educational institution can afford to lose sight of 'discipline' as a form of basic conduct by everyone.

Human Resource Management (HRM) deals with the people dimension of the management of the organization and is necessarily taught to the management students as a compulsory and a core subject. There could be a very strange situation where a student may ask the faculty if all the HR concepts being taught to the student are being practiced in that very institution itself, in the first place.

In our study, management faculty felt that there was a wide gap between preaching HR practices to their students and actually practicing them in their institutes in more than 50 per cent of the cases. The reasons as articulated by various faculty members during the survey are:

- HR is not an important function as perceived by the managements
- Anybody, specially the Head or Admin department can attend to HR issues
- Never realized that there is a gap between preaching and practicing HRM and that it needs to be bridged.

Proper communication flow between Head, faculty and admin staff creates an atmosphere, what could be called a 'school's climate'. When the Head's behaviour with faculty and interaction among faculty is different, it changes the school's climate accordingly. Halpin and Croft identify certain dimensions of behaviours of both faculty and of the Institutional Head that have a bearing on the school's climate.

The faculty could remain 'disengaged' by just going through the motions, with the feeling that the Head is hindering rather than helping in discharging their duties. This happens when the Head keeps himself 'aloof', formal and impersonal and insists for'results' on come what may basis. This leads to a climate of 'indifference' among all employees of the school. Alternatively when the Head attempts to motivate faculty through personal examples and treats them with human touch, the faculty responds with high morale and a sense of accomplishment displaying friendly social relations with each other. This state of affairs lead to an 'Open Climate' which is the most ideal one for any educational institute more so to a business school, as the classrooms have to necessarily become effective centres of learning with no compromise whatsoever. The students become ambassadors of the school once they join the industry; there is a striking co-relation between schools' climate and subsequent performance of the students in the companies. Thus a business school needs to become an effective organization ensuring

- Open climate
- Fearless and free flow of communication
- Clarity of goals as per SMART mnemonic (as discussed in PMS Chapter 7)
- Participation by all in change management and decision making
- Sound teaching and learning with cordial interpersonal relations among faculty
- Effective leadership
- Continuous monitoring and evaluation

"Of all the different factors which influence the quality of education and its contribution to national development, the quality competence, and character of teachers are undoubtedly the most significant. Nothing is more important than securing high quality recruits to the teaching profession, providing them with the best possible preparation and creating satisfactory conditions of work in which they can be fully effective." (Report of the Education Commission 1964–66)

A management teacher has a significant role to play in making the school effective. Apart from disseminating business related knowledge and teaching its application techniques he needs to discharge the following additional responsibilities.

- ***As a Manager:*** Managing his class, students, teaching, evaluation, resources and time, etc.
- ***As a Trendsetter:*** Practicing what he is preaching

- ***As a Facilitator:*** To help students in drawing out their inner talents
- ***As a Leader:*** Adopts a 'come along' approach and not 'go there' or ordering mode.

In short he has to don the mantle of an Friend, Philosopher and Guide (FPG) to a student so as to ultimately become a 'Role Model' for him.

Now the question arises as to how one goes about in ensuring sound morale, high motivation levels among faculty and thus creating an open organizational climate. A close attention to the following is essential:

- Fair recruitment and selection methods
- Equal pay and opportunities
- Professional development facilities
- Fearless flow of communication (up and down)
- Encouragement of new and innovative ideas
- Fair promotional and growth avenues
- Social interactions involving family members
- Establishment of effective grievance handling procedures and conflict resolution systems
- Non-discrimination policies
- Creation of family like atmosphere
- Hand holding in personal crisis situations
- 'One on One' interaction of the faculty with HOD/ Institutional Head on quarterly/half yearly basis
- Carrying out 'Culture Audit' or 'Morale Survey' periodically and addressing the weak areas
- Maintaining cordial relations with the alumni and ex-faculty members
- Encouraging a 'sense of humour' in day-to-day activities
- Centralized morning or evening tea sessions at least once in a fortnight at HOD and Institutional Head level
- Informal discussions on social topics

- Allocation of space for family members in newsletters of the school
- Mentoring of juniors by seniors
- HR Calendar or HR web page.
- Celebrating birthdays and wedding anniversaries of faculty members.

Thus the list could be endless; the aim should be to see a smile on everybody's face at all times.

CULTURE AUDIT OR MORALE OR SATISFACTION SURVEY

A 'Culture Audit' or a Morale or a Satisfaction Survey is a valuable organizational assessment tool to feel the pulse of the individual first and then of the organization as a whole, apart from being an effective upward communication instrument. It should hinge around the following:

Leadership

- Style and Governance
- Vision and Mission

Academic Areas

- Teaching and Learning
- Curriculum
- Evaluation
- Students (Past and Present)

Professional Development

- Research and Publication facilities
- Training and Development
- Coaching and Mentoring programs
- Career Advancement
- Performance Management Systems
- Compensation and Reward Management
- Authority (Identity), Role Clarity and Responsibility

Support Functions

- Working Environment and Infrastructural Facilities
- Trust and Conflict Resolution
- Job Security
- Interpersonal Relations and Communication
- Decision Making and Change Management
- Encouragement for Innovation
- Social Interactions (Events and Celebrations)
- Industry Interface
- Recreational Facilities
- Institution Building Avenues

Above Culture Audit could be conducted as a 'brain storming session' once or twice in a year where faculty should be allowed to express their views freely and suggestions offered if any may be considered actively. The outcome of such considerations must necessarily be informed to the concerned faculty failing which he/she loses faith in the organization and may never offer any suggestions during their remaining stay in the school. Alternatively a 'morale survey' may be carried out by administering a structured questionnaire, a sample of which is given at Annexure I to this chapter. Yet another method is either to use the construct proposed by Udai Pareek in the form of Motivational Analysis of Organizations-Climate (MAO–C) or 'the structured 4-point scale questionnaire to measure organizational climate' developed by TV Rao.

SUMMING UP

The quality of work produced by a willing worker vastly differs from that of an unwilling one. An individual with a sound state of morale and high motivation derives pleasure in executing a task which ultimately will result in a top quality output. Similarly a proper and conducive organizational climate fosters brotherhood among the employees creating a family like atmosphere. This in turn boosts the morale and motivation levels of the employees and management faculty are no exception to this bare fact of organizational life.

The analysis on state of 'morale' prevailing in business schools indicates that generally it is of sound order, and the analysis on 'motivation' of faculty in management institutes indicates that they are well motivated to the extent of recommending their organizations to their friends. They also feel that theirs is an equal opportunity organization.

On Organizational Climate, our study indicates that management faculty are happy to come to office every day and they have a different opinion on their feeling at the end of the working day probably because they are not able to derive 'pleasure' out of work life. Though this is a slight aberration from their earlier responses, but the same could be attributed to probably lack of professional challenges and intellectual stimulations etc. which are essential to have a sense of achievement and consequently the pleasure at the end of the day. On socialization issue also, faculty's response was equally divided and it was established that barely 50 per cent feel like bringing their family members to the 'get togethers' organized by the office. About the quality of work life in the organization, faculty was happy. However close to 75 per cent of them have indicated that there is a wide gap between preaching and practicing HR issues.

In sum total, though the analysis indicates that the general state of morale and motivation levels of management faculty are fairly satisfactory but the whole 'Organizational Climate' in the institutes needs to be improved up to the levels as desired by the faculty, with sound HRM practices in place.

Organizational Climate is an offshoot of the state of morale and motivation levels of the faculty. The working environment provided should be monetarily rewarding, professionally challenging, intellectually stimulating and socially pleasing. Institutional heads may in their own way try to achieve this objective.

Annexure I

Morale or Satisfaction Survey

1. Are you happy to be a part of this organization?

   Yes ☐ No ☐ Not sure ☐

2. Would you like to serve here till superannuating?

   Yes ☐ No ☐ Not sure ☐

   If Yes, what motivates you

   ____

   If No, what demotivates you

   ____

3. Do you feel nice and look forward to come to office every day?

   Yes ☐ No ☐ Not sure ☐

4. Do you feel equally nice at the end of the working day?

   Yes ☐ No ☐ Not sure ☐

5. Do you recommend this organization to your friends?

   Yes ☐ No ☐ Not sure ☐

6. Do you think there is enough 'quality' in whatever you do here?

   Yes ☐ No ☐ Not sure ☐

7. Do you bring your spouse and children for 'get togethers' organized by the school?

   Yes ☐ No ☐ Not sure ☐

8. Are you happy about the general 'Quality of life' you have in this organization?

   Yes ☐ No ☐ Not sure ☐

9. You feel that your institution is practicing all the HR issues it is preaching to the students?

   Yes ☐ No ☐ Not sure ☐

10. What are the HR aspects you feel your organization should address to make you feel very happy, satisfied and contended?

    ____

    ____

    ____

Date: ....

Signature: ....

Name: ....

Department: ....

10

Retention and Separation

No microphone will replace them,
No television system will clone them and distribute them,
No scripted lesson will direct and control them,
No voucher system will bypass them.

– Lee S Shulman

Individuals joining an organization need to feel that they are valued and that their contribution will make a difference. It is easy to say that this is happening, but far harder to have concrete evidence of its application (Kaye Thorne and Andy Pellant). Talent and creativity are the two sides of the same coin which are appreciated on their face but rarely understood and effectively nurtured within organizations. Talent development is not paying specific attention to fewer set of people but it is about building on everybody's strengths. It is more concerned with encouraging diversity, creativity and innovation than merely conducting some training classes. Like the way we discussed about organizational climate in the previous chapter, talent retention is nothing but to create an environment where the organization buzzes with energy and people have a sparkle of anticipation when they enter their workplace. Kaye Thorne and Andy Pellant suggest certain measures for retention of people (talent) in the organization which are relevant to mention here.

- Be committed and respect all your human capital
- Encourage and develop diversity within your workforce
- Don't just pay lip service to the concept of talent management but focus on it.

- Demonstrate commitment from the top for retention of talent
- Demonstrate brand and values
- Create an honest and thinking environment
- Identify and recognize talent at all levels and reward accordingly
- Grant freedom to innovate
- Develop coaching and feedback systems
- Create an encouraging environment for the new people to join
- Create internal forums that allow for healthy debate and discussion
- Encourage flexible and imaginative patterns of employments
- Ensure a developing and learning culture
- Be socially responsive

Every employee is talented (our scriptures say *Amantro Aksharo Naasti: Naasti Mulyamsha Aushadham; Ayogyaha Purusham Naasti; Yojakaha Durlabhaha*—meaning, there is no letter which is not a mantra or a lesson, there is no herb or a plant which has zero medicinal value, similarly there is no human being who is absolutely useless) and talent is not a rare thing, it is simply rarely identified and still rarely allowed to release itself. Organizations must strive to create an environment where talent is not exceptional but just normal. Retention will follow on its own.

RETENTION OF MANAGEMENT FACULTY

As we have already discussed in the earlier chapters about management faculty coming under the category of knowledge workers now in the light of above discussion we can also now safely classify them as 'talented workforce'. It is this 'talent' that is put to use to transform a simple student into a highly productive managerial asset to any organization, to that extent we can call every management teacher as a 'talented knowledge worker' (JK Nandi 2005). All the committees on management education in India namely Nanda (1981), Kurien (1992), Ishwar Dayal (2001) and AICTE (2003) were of the singular opinion that one of the major problems in management education in India today is the shortage of faculty. If strategies in management education mean expansion, diversification, industry interface, curriculum development and infrastructure development it also means retention of talented knowledge workers, i.e. faculty members.

In the addition to active recruiting during the hiring process, campuses should be vigilant to identify retention problems that may have a negative impact on faculty diversity and equal employment opportunity. Conducting exit interviews for those who are leaving to ascertain the reasons for their departure is an effective retention tool. This provides an opportunity for understanding obstacles to retention and designing effective responses to the problem so identified. Similarly a faculty who stayed the longest should also be requested to give his reasons that contributed to his long stay. These factors could be reinforced and further strengthened to motivate other faculty members.

Yet another effective tool of retention is the mentoring program for junior faculty as a part of effective campus retention program. Formal mentoring programs, and conducting exclusive workshops and other development programs for the junior faculty would put to rest their misgivings and apprehensions about the organization and contribute to their continued stay in the institute. Many campuses have Faculty Development Programs (FDP) to update the KSA (Knowledge, Skills and Attitudes) base of the faculty which is also another effective faculty retention mechanism. One may come across an excellent faculty who could be considered as an asset to the organization but who has some special needs in terms of flexi day/time to teach. A highly considerate view of such needs would go a long way in bringing about the sense of belongingness in the faculty concerned. Equal pay practices and non-discriminatory policies on account of caste, creed and gender are equally important to retain faculty.

Each campus may promote faculty diversity and equal opportunity by making every effort to provide a scholarly and educational environment that is supportive of all faculty members. Campuses may also provide public and academic recognition to faculty who make exceptional contributions to academic and educational diversity through their research, teaching or service activities. Certain other strategies suggested to be followed for retention of management faculty are (JK Nandi) (University of California)

- Wide publicity and fair recruitment
- Proper induction and orientation
- Monitoring pay equity and benefits at par with the best in the industry (Both monetary and non-monetary)
- Mentoring junior faculty
- Sound infrastructural facilities
- Optimum workload
- Enforcing non-discrimination policy
- Facilities for self-development
- Creating a welcoming campus climate
- Support for consulting work
- Encouraging cross curricular diversity
- Appropriate recognition for institution building
- Satisfaction or morale surveys
- Creating a sense of belongingness
- Performance driven promotional avenues
- Exit interviews
- Rewarding research output and exemplary performance
- Effective post separation HRM care

INDUCTION AND ORIENTATION

First few days in an organization are very crucial both for the new employee and the organization. New employees normally take decision either to stay or to leave the organization in the first one-week only and maximum number of people leave their organization in the first few months only. As such induction and orientation are very important wherein a new employee is taken into the fold, made to feel comfortable, allowed to settle down, familiarized with the job and the organizational set-up, and all this is done before assigning him the actual job. Management faculty are assigned to their departmental colleague for a period of one month or so to acquaint himself with the organizational culture. This training is yet another effective retention tool forming part of the overall retention strategy of the business school.

Induction/orientation training is too important an activity to be either ignored or treated lightly. Specially in case of management faculty who needs to find his bearings in the new surroundings so as to be able to deliver goods at the earliest. Some institutes leave the faculty to organize his own induction, while some others put the new faculty under a senior faculty for a fixed duration during which the new faculty is expected to familiarize himself. Ideally it could be a well documented and organized program of say two to three weeks through which a new faculty is made to go through all facets of the institution before assigning formal teaching load. A proper feedback from the faculty on the induction training received should be made compulsory.

Research carried out by Lars Moratis, Petervan Baalen, Linda Teunter, and Paul Verhaegen in 2005 revealed the factors considered important by the European Business School faculty for their retention are

- Academic Freedom
- Adequate Research Time
- Geographic Location of the School
- Opportunities for Professional Development

This indicates that their pay and perks have been well taken care of while that forms a significant retention factor in our country. A point to be remembered here is that perceptions of the faculty in this aspect are more important than that of the institutional heads.

SEPARATION

Separation of an employee from the organization for one reason or the other is inevitable. But making the employee leave the organization on a happy note is a critical responsibility of the management. This is best achieved by sound HR policies, some of which have been discussed under retention strategies. Firstly every organization should have a proper exit policy specifying the methodology to be adhered to, then the management should settle the terminal benefits of the exiting employee within a specified time, and maintain touch with former employees so as to hire them back should the need so arise. These are only few methods of ensuring smooth and hassle free exit so that employees hold the organization in high esteem and return back whenever they want to. It is a well known fact that a happy employee spreads a good word to about five people, whereas an unhappy former employee talks ill of the organization to at least a hundred odd people. So the significance of sound exit policy cannot be underestimated.

Despite the technological advancement leading to the use of computers the responsibility of shaping the destiny of nations through the minds of younger generations has not been taken away from the teachers nor the same is possible in the perceivable future. Management faculty mould the managers in the making. Like in any other teacher–student relationship, an even stronger emotional bond gets established between a management faculty and his student. This bond further gets strengthened with the rising career graph of the student ("Look, he was my student, I am proud of him," one often hears management faculty saying) and frequent-alumni interactions through newsletters, emails, and get-togethers. Under these circumstances separation of a management faculty from the institute for any reason whatsoever is a painful thing. Like they say 'what cannot be cured must be endured' so is the case with the exit of a faculty from the system. However, if the same process is undertaken on a pleasant note both the organization and the faculty would benefit as the chances of faculty coming back (in case of lateral move) may become brighter. Certain measures (based on the study and the experience of the researcher) to ensure smooth exit of the faculty are:

- Counseling
- Ascertaining reasons for lateral move
- Providing chances to reconsider decision by redressing grievances if any
- Formal exit interviews at technical, administrative (HR) and institutional head levels.
- Keeping options open for hiring back
- Filling up a staff separation/exit form*
  (*A suggested format is attached as Annexure I to this chapter)
- A formal farewell function
- Presentation of a momento
- Settling terminal benefits preferably on the last working day of the faculty (Indian Railways is reported to have achieved this unique distinction)

SUMMING UP

It has been estimated that there is a need for over 4000 trained faculty in management education if all recognized schools are to meet the minimum norms (7 per institute as per AICTE norms). This is without counting the large number of private institutes who operate either on their own or who form part of private universities under State Legislatures, and also those existing faculty who need to be separately trained in teaching management students. Most come into management classrooms with no background except in their own subject but have had no exposure as to how they must tailor their teaching to fit management teaching (SL Rao 2005). This shortage of faculty is likely to swell to astronomical figures if we consider the ideal and desired teacher student ratio as 1 : 10, for all the business schools across the country. All said and done, management faculty shortage is a serious problem world over and is a much bigger problem for our country.

In these days of critical shortages of qualified and talented management faculty, retention strategies and harmonious separation techniques assume a lot of importance and no business school can afford to lose sight of these vital functions. The shortages are so heavy in number that it is almost impossible to make them up in the near future. Hence the academic and functional wisdom for business schools lie in retaining the existing talent and hiring back the former faculty.

The analysis of data collected through our research shows that majority of the management institutes do not have an exclusive HR functionary to handle HR issues. Also only few schools conduct induction and orientation programs and even still fewer conduct exit interviews. In sum total it can be said that the retention strategies followed by business schools need to be improved significantly specially in areas like properly handling all HRM related issues by a suitable HR functionary and having formal induction and orientation programs, etc. Similarly in the separation process it was observed that a formal exit policy does exist only in just 14 per cent of business schools researched and it takes a long time for an exiting faculty to get his terminal benefits. The lackadaisical attitude of the managements towards an exiting/exited employee though not articulated as such by the faculty for obvious reasons but was generally implied so, during interactions of the researcher with the faculty. Also business schools do follow the system of hiring the former employees back, only in few cases. Thus on the 'separation' issue it can be inferred as that, business schools need to affect improvements on their faculty exiting process.

Both from our study/research and study of highly focused survey reports the following recommendations are made for the retention of faculty in management institutes.

- The prevailing atmosphere should encourage academic freedom, new initiatives and innovativeness and must have reputation among academic and business fraternity.
- The conditions of employment must provide job security, be financially and non-financially rewarding, and also ensure a fair balance between work and life.
- The working culture should ensure personal and professional development through family involving initiatives and opportunities for professional growth and cross disciplinary scholarship.
- A stimulating teaching climate which is both intellectually challenging and professionally rewarding is essential. Similarly, adequate facilities and due encouragement for taking up research are the critical needs.
- The quality of infrastructure and the quality of students, both contribute to passionate teaching.
- Proper 'exit policy' must exist in management institutes so that 'separation' of faculty for any reason becomes mutually pleasing.
- Business Schools should not 'shy away' from the practice of 'rehiring' the ex-faculty.
- 'Induction and orientation' programs must necessarily be conducted in all business schools.
- A suitable HR functionary should be put in place to take care of all HR needs of the faculty on a proactive basis.
- Let us not forget the fact *"in hell there is no retention".* (Miguel de Cervantes Saavendra)

Annexure I

Staff Separation/Exit Form

(**Note:** This form may be filled up by faculty either during service or while separating from the institute. The form may be dropped in the drop box outside Director's office.)

1. Designation: .... 2. Date of Joining: ....
3. Present CTC ₹: .... 4. Expected CTC ₹: ....
5. Comment on working environment/organizational culture.

   ____

   ____

   ____

6. Comment on your relationship with your boss.

   ____

   ____

   ____

7. Comment on the learning, development, promotional avenues.

   ____

   ____

8. Specific reasons for leaving the organization (other than mentioned above).

   ____

   ____

9. Do you consider coming back at a later date – Yes/No?
   If No, elaborate ______________________________________

10. Have you enjoyed your work and interaction with students – Yes/No?
    If No, elaborate ____

11. Any other comments/suggestions you would like to make for the general improvement of the organization.

    ____

    ____

    ____

    ____

11
Leadership and Governance

"People seldom improve when they have no other model but themselves to copy."

– Oliver Goldsmith

There is no denial of the fact that leadership by example is the most effective of all styles. A child learns a lot of leadership lessons from her parents at home as confirmed by a study by HBR. Leadership as a concept had fascinated theorists all over the world for many years now and it still continues to do so. Leadership is defined in many ways depending on the meaning one assumes to it. Some may consider it as power while for others it could be plain charisma. Stephen Robbins aptly puts it 'the ability to influence people towards achievement of goals'. Warren G. Bennis considered as an authority on leadership observes "to survive in the twenty first century; we are going to need a new generation of leaders—leaders, not managers". Because leaders fight through the adverse situations and turbulent environment while managers, as the belief goes generally, tend to surrender to them. Leadership unlike management is much broader in its scope encompassing strategy, infectious enthusiasm and sheer sincerity of purpose, from whom the leader draws power. People follow the leader out of total respect and esteem as their values and aspirations get reflected by him only. In the last half of a century or so there has been a virtual flood of leadership theories with all kinds of adjectives used. But just as a Chinese proverb goes "routes to a mountain are many but view from the top is always the same", similarly, all great leaders have lots of common traits though subtly differ in some. Like, they all are, visionaries, thinkers, doers, result oriented, empathizers, personal examples setters, generous with praise, and last but not the least is that they are teachers practicing what they preach. Yes, we are talking about teachers the intellectual leaders, as the builders of any nation if we succinctly put it.

TRANSFORMATIONAL LEADERSHIP

If your actions inspire others to dream more, learn more, do more and become more, you are a leader.

– John Quincy Adams

Classic studies of educational institutions (Halpein 1966) describe their leadership as providing 'structure' and 'consideration' dealing with the hard and soft parts of the system respectively. Effective institutional leaders pursued mainly two goals: passing knowledge from one generation to the next and turning out good citizens who are useful to the society. To that extent, the sole task of any educational institution in any country is to support the harmonious and total development of its student population inculcating a sense of curiosity and a strong desire to learn. Effective leaders make their group members less interested in themselves and more in the group (Burns 1978). Studies have indicated that transformational leadership is synonymous with effective leaders. The process of transformational leadership involves inspiration, consideration and stimulation (Kane, Tremble, Koh et al. 1995, 2000) with which group's commitment and motivation are closely associated. It is through their charisma and inspiration, transformational leaders provide a clean sense of purpose and mission to their followers who in turn develop a sense of loyalty and commitment. Yet another dimension is the developmental process put in place by suitable delegation of projects and assignments by the leaders to the followers to enhance their learning skills. Finally, it is the innovative and creative bent of mind on the part of transformational leader himself that intellectually stimulates his followers, to adopt 'out of the box' approach as against, the conventional and the established.

Effective leadership is an essential ingredient for social development and prosperity and institutions of learning contribute enormously to this developmental process and in creating leaders for a diverse society. Leadership as a tool has the power to transform people due to its sheer impact on the people and the events. Research studies have indicated that 'there are reasons to believe that leaders are neither born nor made but the capacity to lead is inherent in every individual and all it needs is the right reason and situation to manifest itself'. Today's world is full of turbulences in terms of global challenges, concerning religion, environment, wealth distribution, ineffective governance and over emphasis on knowledge, etc. To cope up with this dynamic and ever emerging national and world trends, future leaders not only require knowledge and skills but also emotional maturity and spiritual wisdom. Students and teachers need to see, feel and acknowledge the leadership of their leader as a part of their education to become leaders themselves. If the students are to become useful members of the society they must be exposed to similar contribution by the institution they study in. In this context, the institutional leadership assumes special significance.

Qualities that are expected to be possessed by an intellectual and institutional leader are:

Intellectual/Institutional Leader

- ***Self-awareness:*** Ability to recognize one's own feelings, values, beliefs, attributes, emotions and limitations and how they affect self and others and of all the adaptability to change and transform.
- ***Integrity:*** By far the most valuable asset of a leader which indicates the consistency of actions with values and beliefs. This is the only factor that acts as a bridge of trust between leader and his followers.

- ***Sense of commitment:*** This is the driving force that motivates people to push ahead even in trying circumstances. It is the culmination of traits like passion, intensity, sincerity, persistence and a strong will to do and to achieve.
- ***Empathy:*** The ability to feel the pulse of others or simply said 'the art of listening to and understanding others' view points'. Very few leaders possess this noble trait despite its critical need.
- ***Knowledge and skill:*** No leader can be effective without possessing the requisite knowledge, skills and the technical expertise. His personal credibility should be established beyond doubt through his competence; otherwise, the transformation efforts would go waste on his followers.
- ***Expect more:*** It is generally seen that a highly demanding environment acts as a powerful stimulus in performance. However the leader himself should set personal examples in this regard, at the same time not losing the sight of accepting 'achievable and reasonable' performance from his followers though there would be some who deliver more than expected.
- ***Leadership building skills:*** No leader is considered as a real leader unless he is engaged in the serious business of developing leaders. This is ensured in a group by creating a collaborative and learning environment, establishing commonalities of purpose, ensuring freedom of thought, action and expression and emphasizing mutual regard, and respect for each other's contribution.

Student Leaders

Leadership development even for students is no less a critical factor as these are to build a better society in future. This is also important from the fact that it gives them a greater sense of control over their careers and lives. Few suggested measures to ensure this development include:

- Head of the institution and the teachers becoming role models for students by practicing what they preach or teach.
- Engaging students in off-classroom activities in groups to strengthen overall campus climate
- Encouraging students to participate in community service activities, etc.
- Drawing out the supposedly shy and weak, emphasizing the fact that leadership is not the sole prerogative of the privileged few.
- Driving repeatedly the point home, that it is the students who make the institution and not faculty or buildings.
- Ensuring core principles of leadership discussed herein, permeate the student culture resulting in a 'transformed' campus.

Faculty Leaders

Teaching is a noble profession which happens more out of choice than of chance. People pick it up for the sheer 'joy of teaching', opportunity to interact with students and to participate in shaping society's next generation (AHE survey – Rice, 1996). With the powerful influence they have over their pupils, teachers become leaders in their own right without being formally so. This leads to the situation where they become friend, philosopher, guide, mentor, and coach and finally a role model to a number of students. Unfortunately, many faculty members restrict themselves to mere classroom teaching that too on a traditional monologue style (take it or leave it basis), which cannot help the students even to become good followers leave alone becoming good leaders. The principles of transformative leadership discussed above are equally applicable to faculty as they are to the head of the institution or to the students per se. Because it is the faculty who act as the channels of societal transformation. Again as members of the research groups, faculty members foster their interpersonal relations and skills which by itself is a practice of transformative leadership.

Like the traditional rivalry between the staff and line functions of any organization, faculty of an educational institution generally tends to develop mistrust in the administration, and vice versa. In the process, the students get sandwiched and bear the brunt. Following excerpt from a US national report illustrates this.

"The faculty don't trust administration. Student's find faculty distracted and not well attuned to their learning needs, administrators are wary of both trustees and faculty. Staff sees themselves as disenfranchised victims of administration's need to save money and the faculty's penchant for protecting their own. Frequently, schools, departments, and even individual faculty act as if they are each other's targets."

– Pew Policy Perspectives, May 1997, Volume 7, Number 2

Lack of trust creates a 'we – they' mentality and with this, faculty members rarely or never get involved in institutional image building activity. There is a dire need for the teaching fraternity to recognize the contribution of non-teaching staff like counselors, placement services or administrative services as they also clearly interact with students and impart valuable life lessons to them, in no less measure.

GOVERNANCE

"to promote knowledge and integrity in the art of finance, industry and commerce ..."

– Vision of HBS, as inscribed on a tablet in Baker Library, HBS

Governance of an institution is a shared responsibility between the administration, faculty and the students and all are stakeholders. Hence a unified and a synergetic approach is what is called for. Apart from teaching and other scholastic pursuits faculty needs to focus on the following:

- Academic administration (admission, curriculum delivery and exams)
- Students' co-curricular and extra curricular activities
- Students' character and personality building activities
- Industry interface through seminars and conferences, consultancy and MDP and EDPs
- Research and publications
- Peer group activities (selection, reviews and mentoring)
- Being a student and learner himself all through
- Any other institution image building activity assigned from time to time by the management.

The general belief prevailing among faculty that they are the 'core or the centre' of the institution and that the institution could not survive without them often acts as a weakness to their strengths, which undermines the collaboration process. Excessive autonomy normally results in misuse of power while one can use it to strengthen one's commitment to the institution. It needs no further emphasis that faculty have the power to change, to transform, to metamorphose the younger generation for the better, and by practicing the principle of transformative leadership they can initiate the process of creating an institution and a society which would be a far better place to live.

REGULATORY OR GOVERNANCE MECHANISM

For business schools coming under the purview of AICTE through NBA and UGC through NAAC the government rules and regulations apply.

But most of the private business schools whether coming under the fold of AICTE or UGC or not, are run either as 'not for profit' or as 'profit driven' organizations. In either of the cases, they do not depend upon the government for any funding and their internal accruals mainly consisting of fee from students, sale of publications, books, case studies, and consultancy/EDP assignments help them to sustain themselves. To that extent they are autonomous in their functioning and with the ever increasing demand for management education there are adequate reasons to believe that number of business schools generate substantial surpluses. Thus there is a dire need for an effective internal governing mechanism in terms of Boards of Management, or Advisory Boards or both. While Boards of Management are responsible for the overall efficient functioning of the business school. Advisory Boards limit themselves to reviewing curricula, industry's expectations from the academia, the quality of student output and rankings. Both the boards must have adequate faculty representation, and independent members who have no connection with the promoters and do not benefit in any way other than getting their incidental expenses reimbursed. Finances must be audited regularly and the details must be made public. Policy regarding use of surpluses must be laid down and followed religiously by the boards.

The general opinion of experts in the field is there should be a separate regulatory body for management education in the country and all management programs and institutions must function under it as one unified authority.

INSTITUTION BUILDING

Udai Pareek in his treatise 'Beyond Management' (Oxford & IBH Publishing Co.Pvt. Ltd 1994) defines institution building as the "process of establishing or transforming an organization into an integrated and organic part of a community in a way that will help the organization play a proactive role in projecting new values and becoming an agent of change in the community". Simply saying this would mean establishing an institution and nurturing it through various stages successfully. A business school head even if he was not involved in establishing it, has an obligation to steer its growth through various developmental processes. The learned author puts forward certain propositions to the leader to ensure institution building.

- Devote full time and attention to the institution
- Take pride in the development of each employee
- Respect the roles others play and provide autonomy
- Establish linkages and attend to the external affairs
- Be prepared to learn and change
- Learn to be dispensable and dispossessive

All time great institution builder Ravi J Matthai focuses on self-regulation as the key to institution building (Beyond Management: Udai Pareek Oxford & IBH 1994) highlighting on the following attributes of the leader:

- Foster and sustain self-discipline among faculty by instilling a sense of responsibility in every task assigned
- Encourage autonomy and creativity
- Not to 'use' the institution but to 'build' it
- Not to be dependant on the job
- To be more an effective part of the continuum rather to be regarded as a great institution builder at the end of the tenure

(Ravi J Matthai was the first full time Director IIM-A during the period 1965–72 and then continued as a professor till his death in 1986. He created and nurtured a professional and peer group culture, and sustained the self-renewing process in the institute.)

STUDENT SERVICES (NON-TEACHING) STAFF: HRM NEEDS

In addition to the faculty, there are so many members of institutional staff who interact with the students in their day to day activities. As such, they have an important role to play in shaping and molding the personalities of students. For a student, everybody in the institution is a teacher (formal and informal) and he tends to pick up things (good or bad) during his various interactions with them. There again is a general tendency among the student services staff to shy way from instilling transformational leadership qualities among the students under the pretext of not holding any formal position of authority. They normally consist of academic coordinators, hostel wardens, general administrators, counselors, soft skills trainers, placement and industry interface personnel and public relations and event managers, etc. In fact, if one half of learning takes place inside the classroom, the other half comes to the students from these student services personnel. In a way they educate the students for their holistic development . There is a need to convince them of this strong belief to prevent them from their self-limiting professional behaviour which by itself is detrimental to development of leadership qualities in a student. Authenticity, integrity and commitment are the key qualities these personnel are expected to possess while playing their transformational leadership roles.

By far the most neglected staff in an educational institution are the non-teaching/sub-staff, staff, more aptly referred as 'the unsung heroes'. Management institutes are no exception to this general apathy prevailing in campuses. Compared to support or staff function of a business enterprise while as knowledge workers faculty are equated with the line staff, members of non-teaching staff leave no stone unturned in making sure that the faculty delivers and the student receives, whatever is intended and expected. Without them the faculty would be like soldiers without weapons. Be it in keeping the premises clean, making the classrooms technically ready for instruction, attending to examination related work, providing library and Internet facilities, attending to various requirements of students, their placements and faculty, etc. they are 'every where' all the time. So much so, the old students of management schools during their alumni meets remember these noble souls more fondly than they do even their faculty members. Their student friendliness and helping attitude make them very popular on the campus. While faculty as 'crying babies' get their milk, it is the silent non-teaching staff that are generally denied their rightful due. Business School head must pay particular attention to the following aspects concerning their HRM needs:

- Periodic rise/revision of compensation.
- Adequate incentives for overtime work. (office boys/ maintenance staff/drivers etc.)
- Providing growth and self-developmental avenues.
- Free education to the wards.
- Provision of uniforms or allowances in lieu of.
- Accessibility to all facilities of the institution.
- Suitable PMS in place with performance based incentives.
- Strict compliance of all statutory provisions as applicable.

The fact is 'they also serve' and are as important as anybody else in the organization and deserve to be treated as such.

HEAD OF THE BUSINESS SCHOOL

The list of functions, the head of an academic institution is expected to perform is long and diverse though there is no generally accepted job description. Briefly they may include budgeting, fund raising, consultancy, public relations, planning, mediation, staff development, articulating a vision, crisis management and consensus building, etc. and the list is endless. Some may require PR skills, others ask for administrative or organizing skills but mostly the requirement is of leadership skills—intellectual and transformational. Virtually, all heads of higher educational institutions nurture some dreams for their institutions concerning its growth and development. At the outset, he should articulate this vision to his staff, faculty, students, trustees, industry, alumni and to society in general. Having done that, the leadership principle of 'authenticity' has to flow down from the top, to gain trust and support of his followers. His own 'self-awareness' and competence help him in facing the pressures, both internal and external. He could even consider forming a 'core group' (consisting of HODs and his immediate deputy) to assist him in affecting institutional changes or transformation. Some of the suggested actions that are likely to help the head of a business school in his intellectual or transformational leadership roles are:

- Transparency in all dealings
- Mutual trust
- Regular interactions with staff, faculty and students both official and social
- An occasional teaching interaction (formal or informal) with students
- Encourage research culture through self-participation (could be notional)
- Take up publication activity once in a while
- Ability to take and carry the team along
- Empathy and mutual respect
- Industry interaction and reforms in academic curriculum
- Disciplining students
- Eye on the budget and the costs.
- Though 'not seen' but to be 'felt' all the time by the staff, faculty and students
- Deep concern for the welfare and morale of the staff, faculty and students
- Exhibit and expect innovation and creativity in running the institution and tap the intellectual talents.
- Let 'criticism' not act as a deterrent in the development process
- Cultivate the art of 'listening'.
- Excellent PR skills and institution image building capabilities.
- Taking adequate care of HRM needs of both academic and non-teaching staff

In short, the head of the institution is a kind of a torch bearer under whose light faculty, staff and students trace their steps placing one after the other, and that is what intellectual or transformational leadership is all about.

"Never doubt that a small group of thoughtful committed citizens can change the world; indeed it's the only thing that ever has."

– Margaret Mead

Now we consider it essential that a model of a typical business school is suggested to answer the question as to what is to be led and governed. This is given at Annexure I to this chapter.

BUSINESS SCHOOL LEADERSHIP: A NEW DIMENSION

These days not a day passes without our HRD ministry appearing in the media on the reforms in education sector. A point to note is the state of deemed universities in the country and the controversies surrounding them. Against this backdrop, business management education in the country is turning a new leaf. As the academic year approaches, newspapers are full of advertisements on opening of new business schools.

Though the exact number of business schools in the country as on date is anybody's guess, rough estimates put it as in excess of 2000 and increasing, a sizeable figure by any standards. While some fall under the approved by AICTE or UGC category, yet few others are entirely on their own stream emphasizing on 'quality' as their main stay. Howard Thomas of Warwick Business School, Coventry, UK, in his paper "an analysis of the environment and competitive dynamics of management education" analyzes the future roles and strategic choices open to business school heads using a PEST (political, economic, social and technology) framework. Though the study was on European business schools, but relevance of certain issues raised cannot be ruled out in Indian context too, more so in the presently prevailing circumstances where 'education' has become a hot topic of national debate on daily basis. Let us examine the PEST framework first.

Political

Regulatory bodies like AICTE and UGC must bring all the business schools under their fold to ensure standardization and uniformity. Subsequently business schools could go in for AACSB, EFMD, AMBA or SAQS accreditation for their programs. The newly constituted body National Council for Higher Education and Research – by HRD ministry could look into teaching and research quality being undertaken in these schools. Private operators should be encouraged with corresponding reduction in governmental or public funding of business management education, through IIMs, IITs or Universities.

Economic

With trend towards globalization and free trade increasing and India and China emerging as 'growing economies' of the world there is a big demand for quality management education so much so that number of foreign players are knocking at our doors to open their branches here. Banks are coming forward to offer loans liberally to the aspiring students.

Social

The importance of 'ethics' as a societal value is increasing with Satyams and Enrons, cropping up with unfailing regularity. Yet another concern is of environment and the associated precautions in the interest of the future generations. Also more and more working executives, older and more experienced and ladies with children, from diverse backgrounds are coming to management classrooms. Thus management education as a preferred choice of higher education by all and sundry needs no further emphasis.

Technology

With the rapid advancement in technology, there is a strong need to leverage on it by blending the classroom teaching with web based dissemination of knowledge. The advent of Internet has brought in a kind of revolution with knowledge flood gates getting opened with the flick of a button.

Certain challenges that are likely to be faced by the present day business school heads:

- Older students from across diverse cultures with work experience have different learning needs as compared to those coming from undergrad courses, to that extent, customized and more flexible approaches may have to be developed.
- Today's management graduates need to have skills *(flexibility, cultural sensitivity and integrity topped the list of 40 managerial attributes in a survey carried out by Laura Tyson, Dean of London Business School on 100 global executives)* and training to compete in the new economy defined by liberalization, privatization and globalization. There is a strong need to review the curricula regularly and continuous updating of knowledge and skills by the faculty would become a survival factor for the school.
- Entrepreneurship and 'family run businesses' getting a boost and the need to prepare students to make a foray into them and make a difference.
- Rising costs of management education and entry of large number of private operators including foreign players (in the form of FDI) into the field.
- Meeting the ever growing shortage of professionally qualified and academic faculty (Cranfield boasts of 90 per cent of their faculty having real business experience) and addressing their 'compensation' related issues, which is specific to our country as highlighted in Chapter 8.
- Balancing the twin hurdles of academic rigour and practical relevance (Pettigrew 1997), by broadening the roles of research and of pedagogy.

Thus the business school head of today has a challenging task ahead in organizing and reconfiguring his school, to play a vital role in the context of new and emerging economies and knowledge society.

CASE STUDY

RANKING RACE

Background

Mr. C.K. Reddy an IIM alumni and a person with vast industry experience of three decades is the Dean of Excellent Business School (EBS), Hyderabad. He is ably assisted by Colonel Rao, a war veteran, full of beans who handles both academics and administration with equal ease. In between them they also handle marketing and HR courses respectively for the students so as to remain in touch with the subject and with the students. The school established in the year 1995 is very popular among a network of eight such schools across the country and offers PGDM program on autonomous mode which has a wide acceptance in the industry. The school located in the commercial hub of the city of Hyderabad functions from a rented premises spread over a few adjacent buildings to cater to the increasing number of students with every passing year. The school has a fairly good faculty both visiting/adjunct and permanent though other infrastructural facilities are inadequate. But the faculty has the advantage in terms of intellectual development, through publication and research as the EBS network is a major component of an organization called Forum for Professionals in Management (FPM) who carved a niche for themselves in offering higher education programs in various disciplines of management having made a humble beginning in the year 1985. The forum runs publishing houses, case development centres and provides facilities for research and consultancy etc.

The Situation

For the first time ever EBS Hyderabad gets ranked at 31 among business schools of the country in the year 2000, i.e. on completion of five years of standing, by a premier ranking agency of the country. The subsequent 'quarterly review meeting' conducted by the Board of Management is devoted to discussion on these rankings with special focus on each parameter where the school scored low points and the corresponding need to improve upon, not forgetting to compliment the team for the first ever good ranking the school received.

At the end of 3 hours of intensive discussions, Chairman of the Board of Management concludes the meeting by saying "Mr. Reddy, let us find EBS, Hyderabad in the first ten rankings in the next five years. You may take your team into confidence, and let us achieve this objective, and together we can. Let us also meet more frequently on monthly basis to review the situation. Best of luck".

The Result

Prof Reddy and his team go about the task and within next four (not five) years that is, in the year 2004 itself, EBS, Hyderabad gets ranked as the 10th Best B-school in the country and it has not looked back ever since.

POINTS FOR DISCUSSION

1. Outline the various parameters that any good business school ranking agency considers, and the reasons thereof.
2. List the parameters EBS, Hyderabad, would have scored high and low and why.
3. Carry out a SWOT (Strength, Weaknesses, Opportunities and Threats) analysis of EBS, Hyderabad.
4. How did EBS, Hyderabad, go about achieving what it did? Discuss each ranking parameter wise.
5. Draw out a 'successful ranking policy' for a business school. What role could the institutional head have played in the above 'ranking success'?

Annexure I

Suggested Organizational Structure of a Typical Business School

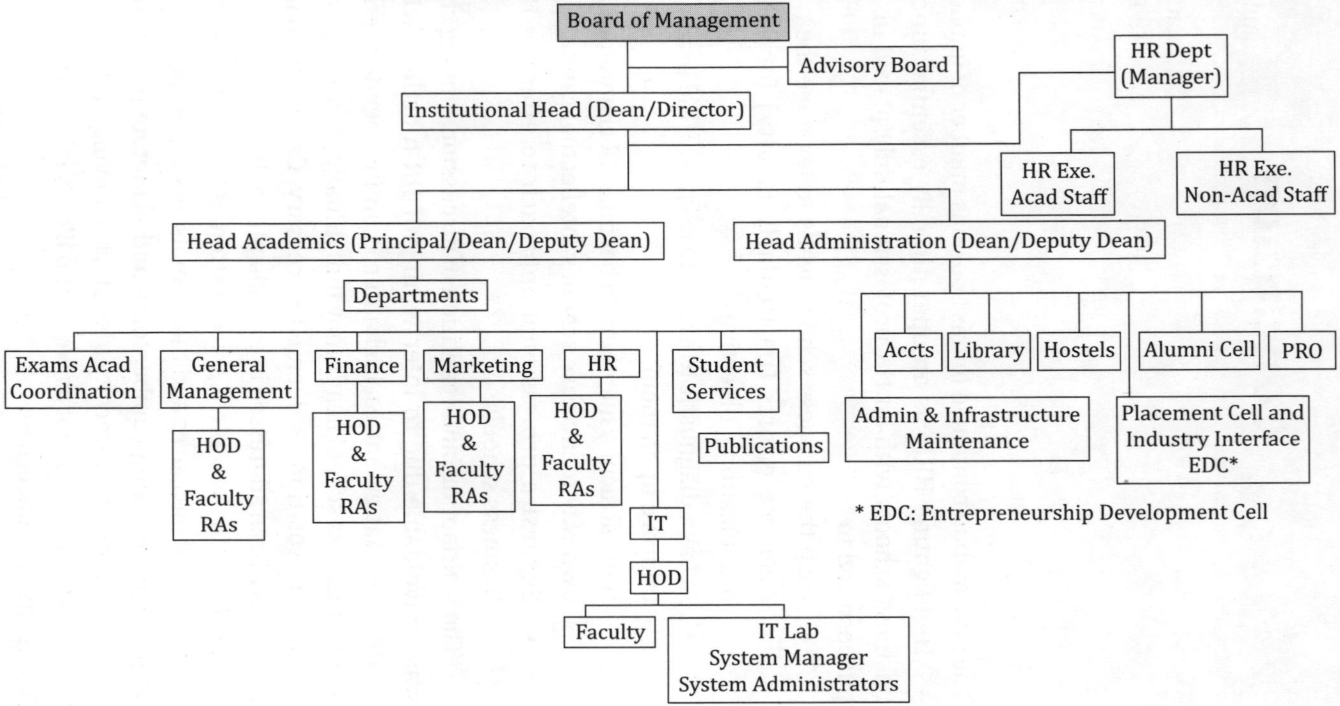

Conclusion

The information contained in this book has number of implications.

Highlighting HRM as an operationally essential function in business schools with an HR professional duly placed in, for the purpose and to

- Help the business school heads to leverage their human resource efforts (particularly faculty) for achieving organizational objectives.
- Act as a diagnostic to evaluate existing HRM practices and improve upon them.
- Help all faculty members to become HR champions in their own way to increase school's intellectual capital
- Suggest a professional approach to effective HRM in business schools.

The overlapping and repetition of discussions among chapters was unavoidable due to intertwining of HR functions with one another, to that extent each chapter is an independent entity by itself. Business school heads may individually refer to a particular chapter in isolation as deemed necessary. Certain fundamental issues have been addressed in each chapter of Part II, only to provide a logical flow to the topic. A sincere attempt has been made to keep the suggested measures and the formats as simple and practicable as possible, avoiding cumbersome and elaborate paperwork. It's time the academic fraternity also start believing in the adage 'see the world as it is, and not as we would like it be' as far as their own HR needs are concerned.

Professor Sterling Livingston in his classical article 'The Myth of the Well Educated Managers' demonstrated the lack of relationship between the grades at the Harvard Business School and subsequent success in management jobs. He argued that business schools need to access intuitive skills and common sense, not just academic ability.

– Dr. Dharni P Sinha – 1995
(Produce Managers not MBAs)

It is sincerely hoped that the book shall achieve its intended objectives.

Bibliography

Books (Partial List)

1. Balasubramanian, *Personnel Management:* Everest Publishing 1999, P. 96.
2. *Best B-Schools Survey 2006: Business India*, October 22, 2006.
3. Bohlander and Snell, *Managing Human Resources: Thomson South western,* 2005, P. 386.
4. Prasad VRK, Reward *Management in Management Schools Education Sector: HR Perspectives,* Vol. I: VRK Prasad (Ed): Icfai Books, 2006, P. 200.
5. Dale Yoder, *Personnel Management and Industrial Relations,* Sixth Edition, Prentice Hall, 1973.
6. Dharni P Sinha, *Management Education in India: Perspective and Challenges,* Icfai Books, 2004, PP. 45–46.
7. Dharni Sinha, *Management Education in India: Perspectives and Challenges,* Icfai Books, 2004, P. 39.
8. Vetter Eric W, *Manpower Planning for High Talent Personnel,* Ann Arbor: The University of Michigan, 1967.
9. Guidelines on Service Matters, *The Institute of Chartered Financial Analysts of India,* P. 4.
10. Faculty of Management Studies, University of Delhi, Delhi, P. 101.

11. Indian Management '*The Best B-School*', Sept. 2005, OUTLOOK India's Top B Schools, Sept. 2005.
12. *Management Education in India: Perspectives and Challenges:* Dharni P Sinha: Icfai Books, 2004, P. 47.
13. Michael Armstrong and Helen Murlis*:* Reward Management *Kogan Page: London and Sterling, First South Asian Edition,* 2005, PP. ix, 2, 4, 5.
14. Andrews N and Tyson LD, The Upwardly Global MBA, *Strategy + Business Issue Reprint No. 04306*, London Business School, London, 2004.
15. Ravi D, *Managing Knowledge Workers—The Bench Marks*, The Management Accountant, November, 2001.
16. Rao SL, *Management Education in India*—AIMA Excel Books, P. 95.
17. Rao TV, *Performance Management and Appraisal Systems* Response Books, 2007, PP. ix, 5, 7, 213.
18. Prasad VRK, '*Management Education in India as an Economy Differentiator*', Enhancing Enterprise Competitiveness: Allied Publishers Pvt. Ltd., Mumbai, 2007, PP. 245–257.
19. Prasad VRK, *Quality Initiatives in Educational Sector with special Reference to Management Education,* Allied Publishers Pvt. Ltd., Chennai, January 2006.
20. *What The Best MBAs Know; Peter Novarro*, Tata McGraw Hill, 2005.
21. *Quality in Service Sector and Managerial Challenges,* Dr. KVM Varambally, Prof. MM Shanbhag, Allied Publishers Pvt. Ltd., Chennai, January 2006.
22. *Research Methodology Methods & Techniques*, CR Kothari, New Age International Publishers.
23. *Strategies for Sustainable Growth: Challenges for Indian Business & Management Education*, Batra JL, Sanjay Srivastava, AIMS.

24. *Human Capital Measurement An Introduction,* Sangeetha K: Icfai Books, 2007.
25. *WTO & Competitiveness: Challenges for Indian Business & Management Education*, Panduranga Rao D, Excel Books, 2001.
26. Agarwal RD, *Dynamics of Personnel Management in India,* Tata McGraw Hill, New Delhi, 1977.
27. Baker MJ and Hart SJ, *Marketing and Competitive Success,* Philip Allan, London, 1989.
28. Beach, Dale S, *Management of People at Work,* Macmillan Publishing Company, New York, 1975.
29. Beard Well and Len Holden, *Human Resource Management,* Macmillan India Ltd, New Delhi, 1996.
30. Special issue of Business Today, '*The Best B-School*', October 18, 2009.
31. OUTLOOK India's '*India's Best B-Schools*', September 28, 2009.
32. Indian Management Special Issue on '*AIMA Survey of Best B-Schools*', October 2009.
33. Udai Pareek, '*Beyond Management*', Second Edition, Oxford and IBH Publishing Company Private Limited, PP. 41–67.
34. Ravi Matthai, Udai Pareek and TV Rao, '*Institutional-building in Education and Research* – from Stagnation to Self-renewal', All India Management Association, New Delhi, 1977, PP. 61–69.
35. David Warner and Elaine Crosthwaite, '*Human Resource Management in Higher Education and Further Education*', published by The Society for Research into Higher Education (SRHE) and Open University Press, Celtic Court, Buckingham, 1998.
36. Dave Ulrich, '*Human Resource Champions: The next agenda for adding value and delivering results*', Harvard Business School Press, Boston, Massachusetts.

37. John M Ivancevich, *'Human Resource Management'*, Tata McGraw Hill Publishing Company Limited, New Delhi, Ninth Edition, 2003.

38. Michael Armstrong, *'Handbook of Human Resource Management Practice'*, Kogan Page Limited, 10th Edition.

39. Wayne F Cascio, *'Managing HR: Productivity, Quality of Work life, Profits'*, Tata McGraw Hill Publishing Company Limited, New Delhi, 7th Edition.

Articles (Partial List)

1. *India and Knowledge Economy: Leveraging strengths and opportunities overviews:* Carldahlman, Anujautz, WBI Development Studies the World Bank Washington DC, Deccan Chronicle, Hyderabad, December 01, 2006.
2. Devika Dharmaraj, *Pre-requisites for an Effective Performance Management System*, NHRD Journal, Feb. 2007, P. 19.
3. *India's Best B-Schools: Business Today*, July 16, 2006, Ishwar Dayal '*Developing Management Education in India*', Journal of Management Research, Vol. 2, No. 2, Aug. 2002.
4. Beck J, *et al.*, "Moving Beyond Team Myths", *Training and Development*, PP. 50, 51–55, 1996.
5. Blasé J and Blasé J, *Empowering Teachers: What Successful Principals Do,* ThousandOaks, Ca: Sage Publications Ltd., 1994.
6. Collins L, "Shared Governance in the California Community Colleges", *Academe*, PP. 88, 36–40, 2002.
7. Fullan M, *"Leadership for the 21st Century: Breaking the Bonds of Dependency", The Josey Bass Reader on Educational Leadership,* PP. 156–163, San Francisco: Josey Bass, 2000.
8. Lucey C, *"Civic Engagement, Shared Governance and Community Colleges", Academe,* PP. 88, 27–31, 2002.

9. McKendall M, *"Teaching Groups to Become Teams"*, *Journal of Education for Business*, PP. 75, 277–282, 2000.
10. Schuetz P, *"Shared Governance in Community Colleges"*, *Eric Digests*, P. 4, 1999.
11. Sergiovanni T, *"Leadership as Stewardship: Who's Serving Who"*, *The Josey Bass Readeron Educational Leadership*, PP. 269–286, San Francisco: Josey Bass, 2000.
12. Allen P, 2003, *"Performance Appraisals with More Gain, Less Pain"*, *Harvard Management Communication Letter*, May 2003, Vol. 6, Issue 3.
13. *Annual Report of University of Tartu* 2002 (2003), University of Tartu.
14. Bjarnason S and Brennan J, *"The Role of Universities in the Transformation of Societies"*, CHERIA/ACU, 2003.
15. Gatfield T, Barker M and Graham P, *"Measuring Student Quality Variables and the Implications for Management Practices in Higher Education Institutions: An Australian and International Student Perspective"*, *Journal of Higher Education Policy and Management*, 21, 2, PP. 239–260, 1999.
16. Levinson H, *"Management by Whose Objectives?" Harvard Business Review*, January 2003, Vol. 81, Issue 1, PP. 107–117, 2003.
17. Longenecker C and Fink L, *"Creating Effective Performance Appraisal"*, *Industrial Management*, 41, 5, PP. 18–26, 1999.
18. McNay I, *"Strategic Planning and Management for Higher Education in Central and Eastern Europe"*, Centre of Higher Education Management, 1997.
19. Willis T and Taylor A, *"Total Quality Management and Higher Education: The Employers' Perspective"*, *Total Quality Management*, 10, 7, PP. 997–1008, 1999.
20. Bolino M and Turnley B, *"Neglected Issues in Citizenship Research"*, In RH Moorman (Chair), *New Frontiers for OCB*

Research: An Examination of Four Research Directions, Symposium Conducted for the Mid-west Academy of Management, St. Louis, MU, 2003.

21. Bulach CR, Malone B and Castleman C, *"An Investigation of Variables Related to Student Achievement", Mid-Western Educational Researcher*, Vol. 8, No. 2, PP. 23–29, 1995.
22. Katz D and Kahn RL, *The Social Psychology of Organizations,* 2nd Ed, New York, Wiley, 1966, 1978.
23. McBrien JL and Brandt RS, *"The Language Learning: A Guide to Education Terms"*, Association for Supervision and Curriculum Development, 1997.
24. Organ DW, *Organizational Citizenship Behavior: The Good Soldier Syndrome,* Lexington, MA, Lexington Books, 1988.
25. Organ DW, *"Organizational Citizenship Behavior: Its Construct Clean-up Time", Human Performance,* No. 10, PP. 85–97, 1997.
26. Regoxs A, *"Citizenship Behaviors of University Teachers: The Graduates' Point of View", Active Learning in Higher Education,* Vol. 4, No. 1, PP. 8–23, 2003.
27. Smith CA, Organ DW and Near JP, 1983, *"Organizational Citizenship Behavior: Its Nature and Antecedents", Journal of Applied Psychology,* No. 68, PP. 653–663.
28. Tripathi, Nachiketa and Chaitanya NK, 2001, *"Dimensions of OCB", Indian Journal of Industrial Relations,* Vol. 37, No. 2.
29. Tschannen-Moran M, *"Collaboration and the Need for Trust", Journal of Educational Administration,* No. 39, PP. 308–331, 2001.
30. Lee S Shulman, *"The Wisdom of Practice: Essays on Teaching, Learning and Learning to Teach",* 2004.
31. David Carr, *Professionalism and Ethics in Teaching,* Routledge, London, 2000.

32. The New Oxford Dictionary of English, Third Impression 2001.

33. *"Teachers' Work and Theories of Professionalism: Conceptualizing a New Approach"*, Presentation at the Annual Convention of the American Educational Research Association, New York, April 8–12, 1996.

34. Mike Bottery, *"The Challenges of Educational Leadership: Values in a Globalized Age,"* Paul Chapman Publishing, a Sage Publications Company, 2004.

35. National Board for Professional Teaching Standards.

36. Devi Laxmi, *Statistical Methods in Social Research,* Amol Publications Pvt. Ltd., New Delhi, 1998.

37. Hackman R and Oldham GR, *"Motivation Throughout the Redesign of Work: Test of a Theory", Organizational Behavior and Human Decision Processes,* Vol. 16, PP. 250–279, 1976.

38. Manikandan P, *"Influential Change Leadership Pattern Among the Faculty Members of Selected State Agricultural Universities", The Icfai Journal of Organizational Behavior,* Vol. 4, No. 3, PP. 7–18, 2005.

39. Pareek Udai, *Training Instruments in HRD and OD,* 2nd Edition, Tata McGraw Hill Publishing Company Limited, New Delhi, 1986.

40. *"Managing B-Schools Better; An Agenda for Reforming Management Education",* J Philip, *Indian Management,* January 2007.

41. *NAAC to become must for colleges:* DC correspondent, Deccan Chronicle, Hyderabad, December 13, 2009.

42. *Teaching is still a thankless job:* Madhurima Chatterjee, Deccan Chronicle, Hyderabad, December 17, 2009.

43. J Scott Armstrong, *Business School Prestige – Research versus Teaching,* published in *Interfaces,* 24 (2), March–April, 1994, PP. 13–43.

44. SL Rao, Management Education, *Missing the Mark,* Indian Management, February 2009.

45. Chandra M Chakravartula and Partha P Sengupta, Human Resource, *Beyond B-School,* Indian Management, September 2009.

46. Stan J Liebowitz, University of Texas at Dallas, *The Role of Research in Business School Rankings,* March 11, 2003.

47. Shyam Sunder, Yale School of Management, *Building Research Culture,* China Journal of Accounting Research, Vol. I, Issue 1, 2008.

48. Business Schools & Research, *Practically Irrelevant,* Economist, August 28th 2007.

49. *Reinventing education:* The Economic Times, Hyderabad, December 17, 2009.

50. Md Moazzam Husain and Abu Mohammad Atiqur Rahman, *Faculty Development in Business Schools: A Global Perspective vis-à-vis Bangladesh Scenario*, Pakistan Journal of Social Sciences, 3 (3): PP. 405–411, 2005, Grace Publications.

51. Howard Thomas, *Business School Strategy and the metrics for success,* Journal of Management Development, Vol. 26, No. 1, 2007, PP. 33–42, Emerald Group Publishing Limited.

52. Robert J Grossman, *Close the Gap between Research and Practice*, November 2009, HR Magazine.

53. Manoj Kumar and Amitabh Deo Kodwani, *Faculty Issues at Business Schools: Challenges and Reconciliation*, Social Sciences Research Network (SSRN).

54. Tritelli D, 2004, P. 3, Editorial Comment, Peer Review, Spring.

55. Howard Thomas, *'An analysis of the environment and competitive dynamics of management education',* Journal of Management Development, Vol. 26, No. 1, 2007, PP. 9–21, Emerald Group Publishing Limited.

56. Rakesh Khurana and Scott Snook, *'A Manifesto for B-Schools',* blog from Harvard Business Review (HBR).

57. Angel Cabrera, *'Let's Professionalize Management',* blog from Harvard Business Review (HBR).

58. Sumantra Ghosal, *'Bad Management Theories are destroying Good Management Practices',* Academy of Management Learning and Education, 2005, Vol. 4, No. 1, PP. 75–91.

59. Sharon Shinn, *'How to Hire',* Biz Ed, November/December 2005.

60. Lars Moratis, Peter Van Baalen, Linda Teunter and Paul Verhaegen, *'Faculty Retention Factors at European Business Schools, How Deans and Faculty Perceptions Differ'*, ERIM Report, RSM Erasmus University, The Netherlands, May 2005.

61. Rebecca M. Bustamante, *'The "Culture Audit": A Leadership Tool for Assessment and Strategic Planning in Diverse Schools and Colleges',* Connexions module: m13691.

Websites (Partial List)

- www.ugc.ac.in
- www.ucop.edu
- www.aicte.ernet.in
- http://www.open.ac.uk/cheri/TRhome.htm
- www.stat.ee
- http://www.bl.uk/pdf/measuring.pdf
- http://www.oclc.org/membership/escan/introduction/default.htm.
- http://www.ssta.sk.ca
- www.collegejournal.com
- http://www.emerald-library.com/brev/04014eg1.htm
- http://deming.ces.clemson.edu/pub/den/qmin_eng-bus.pdf

- http://deming.ces.clemson.edu/pub/den/trans_amer-edu.pdf
- www.aicte.ernet.in
- www.iimahd.ernet.in
- www.iimb.ernet.in
- www.iimcal.ac.in
- http//:www.metu.edu.tr
- www.iimidr.ac.in
- www.iimk.ac.in
- www.iiml.ac.in
- www.learning2004.se
- www.igbp.kva.se
- www.ssrn.com
- www. Economist.com
- www.managementparadise.com
- http://www.informaworld.com
- www.boston.com
- http://cnx.org/content/m13691/1.3/
- www.erim.eur.nl
- www.emeraldinsight.com/0262-1711.htm
- www.exploreHR.org
- http://www.aacsb.edu/publications/Archives/NovDec05/p38-43.pdf
- http://www.egyankosh.ac.in/bitstream/123456789/25714/1/Unit11.pdf.